AUTHOR	CLASS
O'LEARY, M.	623.7463/OLE

TITLE
Bombing twins

04. 02

BOMBING TWINS

ALLIED MEDIUM BOMBERS

BOMBING TWINS

ALLIED MEDIUM BOMBERS

Michael O'Leary

OSPREY
AEROSPACE

First published in Great Britain in 1994
by Osprey, an imprint of Reed Consumer
Books Limited
Michelin House, 81 Fulham Road,
London SW3 6RB
and Auckland, Melbourne, Singapore
and Toronto

© 1994 Michael O'Leary

ISBN 1 855323125

Edited by Tony Holmes
Page design by Paul Kime/Ward Peacock
Partners
Printed in Hong Kong

Front cover Wiley Sanders of Troy, Alabama, must like B-25s – he owns and maintains two of the hungry beasts! Wiley is seen flying *Georgia Mae* while *Ol Gray Mare* keeps a tight formation over Breckenridge, Texas, on 25 May 1991

Back cover Cruising over southern Texas in September 1986 is B-25J *BIG OLE BREW'n little ole you*, which was built for the USAAF as s/n 44-30988. Restored to pristine condition by Tom Reilly at 'Bomber Town', this aircraft was placed in open storage in the late 1980s, whilst its former owner tried to retrieve it back from the Confederate Air Force (CAF), to whom he had earlier donated it. Suffering corrosion problems through neglect, the bomber was transferred to the Southern California Wing of the CAF in July 1993, where it is currently undergoing inspection and repairs to return it to full flying condition

Title page With canopy hatches open, this view gives an idea of the cylindrical shape of the Marauder's fuselage as designed by Peyton Margruder for maximum streamlining

Right Michael O'Leary is seen in the cockpit of a 'bombing twin' of somewhat later vintage – a Lockheed P-2 Neptune being used as a fire bomber by Hawkins & Powers *(Milo Peltzer)*

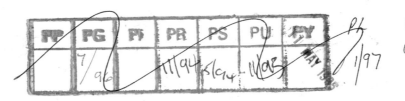

For a catalogue of all books published by Osprey Aerospace
please write to:

**The Marketing Department, Reed Consumer Books,
1st Floor, Michelin House, 81 Fulham Road, London SW3 6RB**

Introduction

The concept of the medium bomber really came into its own in World War 2. During the 1920s, the bomber was basically a rework of World War 1 designs – lumbering biplanes that would have been easy prey for marauding fighters. In the 1930s, the twin-engined bomber really advanced with types like the Martin B-10 and Bristol Blenheim – aircraft that could out-run the majority of contemporary fighters. As Germany began its aggressive military build-up, other countries began a frantic development policy to create more advanced aircraft.

Oddly, it was in isolationist America that the concept of a twin-engine medium bomber really began to mature. Much of this development was spurred by the need of foreign governments for additional aircraft, but American factories churned out tens of thousands of advanced aircraft such as the Ventura, Harpoon, Havoc, Mitchell, Marauder and Invader. Many of the earlier machines were supplied to Britain and France before America entered the war, but after Pearl Harbor the tempo of production rapidly increased and the American concept of the twin-engined medium bomber became the standard.

Bombing Twins has been created to show what these aircraft are like today – precious survivors of a violent time period that are now prized warbirds. We are also presenting a variety of photographs from the last three decades to show how many of these medium bombers were used as work horses after their military careers were over. The fact that some of these aircraft still fly is due to the dedication of their owners and crews, and the fact that the basic designs were incredibly rugged.

The majority of the photographs in *Bombing Twins* were taken on Kodachrome film with Nikon cameras.

Michael O'Leary
Los Angeles, California
July 1993

Right Carl Scholl and Tony Ritzman fly TB-25N USAAF s/n 43-28204 N9856C near Chino during May 1984 while being escorted by Bob Pond in his Grumman F6F-5 Hellcat and Mike DeMarino in The Air Museum's F6F-5. In its distinctive US Navy colours, *Pacific Princess* was finished for many years as a PBJ-1J. Note the open bomb bay doors

Contents

Patrol Bomber

During the 1930s, aviation was 'big box office' for Hollywood. America was 'air minded' and would seem to be willing to spend hard-earned Depression money on just about any film that featured flying. Completed in 1941 and produced on a rather epic scale, the film *Dive Bomber*, starring Errol Flynn, Fred MacMurray and Ralph Belamy, had the usual non-sensical Hollywood plot line of the period but, at over two hours in length, was in glorious Technicolor and featured virtually the entire strength of West Coast naval aviation when all the aircraft were painted in magnificent colour schemes – virtually acres of brilliant, camouflage be damned, warplanes captured permanently on colour stock. Recently released on video, the plot is still silly, but the aircraft make the film worth watching. Prominent among all those aircraft are the US Navy's bright silver and yellow Catalinas with bold squadron markings and codes, clearly illustrating the importance the Navy placed on flying boats. Hack Hollywood biographer Charles Higham would claim in his 1980s book on Errol Flynn that the dashing, but rapidly dissipating, actor was actually a Nazi spy and went out of his way to appear in the film so that he could examine the Navy's aircraft at first-hand for his German masters!

If true, then what the bleary-eyed Flynn would have reported back was

Left With a firm yank on the controls, the captain of this early production PBY-5 breaks away from the camera ship near the Consolidated factory in San Diego, California. Note how the pre-war Catalinas had the bottom of their hulls painted black *(USN)*

Right Several vintage and veteran flying museums operate Catalinas and one of the most active is PBY-6A N7057C (BuNo 64072), owned and operated by the National Warplane Museum in Geneseo, New York. The aircraft was acquired in less than ideal condition and has been an on-going flying restoration for the museum's dedicated volunteers. Photographed on an outing near its home base during August 1989, the aircraft features the housing for an earlier PBY-5A-style nose turret that has been painted over. By 1990, the museum had obtained a late style Catalina nose turret and installed the unit in N7057C. It houses two replica .50 calibre Browning machine guns and features a large blister over the gunner's head for added visibility

that naval aviation was in a woeful state, and inadequately equipped to participate in a major war. True, all those aircraft looked great but, in reality, were obsolete. That fact was true of the Catalina, yet the big boxy flying boat and later amphibian would become one of the true heroes of the war.

Consolidated had enjoyed a long tradition of building patrol bomber flying boats for the US Navy going back to the militarised Commodore airliner of 1928, the XPY-1. Although winning the battle, Consolidated lost the war since Glenn L Martin underbid Consolidated on actual production of the aircraft and thus won the Navy contract. Martin and Consolidated would remain flying boat rivals right up to the final swan song of the type in Navy service.

By 1936, Rubin Fleet had had enough of upstate New York's winters and he moved Consolidated to sunny San Diego, which was also home to a goodly portion of West Coast naval activities. On the way he took his new aircraft, the XPBY-1 and set a long-distance record for seaplanes as the aircraft touched down in the bay next to Lindbergh Field, which would be the company's new home. The XPBY-1 looked *modern* in an Art Deco manner with its pylon-mounted wing, sleek hull, enclosed cockpit and two Pratt & Whitney R-1830-64 Wasps mounted on the wing in tight nacelles. The Navy liked what they saw and placed an order for 60 production standard PBY-1s followed by 50 PBY-2s which featured a slightly modified tail. No one would ever claim that the PBY was a record setter when it came to speed, nor that it was overpowered, but these were turned into virtues

Above With the setting sun reflecting off of N7057C's tri-colour camouflage, the Catalina gracefully descends through the mist for landing

Right The PBY-6A, which derived from the Naval Aircraft Factory PBN-1 Nomad, features an improved hull and wingtip float design. Only 112 PBY-6As were constructed for the US Navy, but a further 75 went to the Army Air Force as OA-10Bs while Russia received 48 under Lend-Lease. This close-up view shows the hull chine to advantage along with the nose gear doors, which must definitely be tightly closed for water landings

because the aircraft had an extremely long range, making it ideal for the patrol bomber role.

Early PBYs, which were given the name Catalina for the attractive island off the southern California coast, were armed with three .30 calibre Browning air cooled machine guns – one in the nose and two in waist hatches. A fourth similar weapon was stored in the hull and could be utilised on a swivel mount firing downward through a hatch in the bottom of the hull. The Catalina could carry a variety of bombs, depth charges, or even two inadequate Mk XIII torpedoes on underwing racks. American aerial torpedoes were notorious for their poor performance and resulted in a scandal during the early days of World War 2, but it took a long while before an efficient American aerial torpedo was perfected.

Consolidated continued churning out a variety of different models of the

Right N7057C is towed back to its parking spot on 16 August 1991 after the successful conclusion of a flight from Geneseo's 'corn field' airstrip, which hosts a large warbird airshow annually. On-going maintenance and restoration work has seen the condition of the PBY-6A improve from year to year and, as it comes available, original military equipment is added to the interior

Catalina for the Navy, the Soviet Union, the odd civilian customer and for the British. On 7 April 1939, the Navy ordered that a PBY-4 flying boat be converted to amphibious gear and the PBY-5A was born – the prototype first flew on 22 November 1939. When the war in Europe began, the Navy could field 224 PBYs in 19 squadrons and since new and improved flying boats were airborne in prototype form or on the drawing board, the Catalina's career seemed limited. However, the Navy soon realised that its need for patrol bombers could be a great one if it was going to have to fight a two ocean war, so in December 1939 it placed a then massive order for 200 PBY-5As. Orders also began to pour in from the Commonwealth nations and Consolidated was forced to expand its factory and hire new employees. The PBY-5A was powered by R-1830-82s and had large waist blisters with two .50 calibre guns, while the nose and tunnel gun remained .30 calibre weapons. It is beyond the scope of this volume to detail the exploits of the Catalina, other than to say that the aircraft was rapidly built and began to engage the enemy from the earliest days of the war – the Navy's Catalina fleet in Hawaii was virtually destroyed by the Japanese attack on 7 December 1941.

American Catalinas began to operate against the enemy from all battle fronts – from steaming jungles to the harsh Aleutians. Even though the aircraft was obsolete in almost every sense, it was also damn effective at destroying shipping and submarines. Britain made effective use of the Catalina by hitting Hitler's U-boats hard in the Battle of the Atlantic and stopping the terrible losses to the convoys bringing supplies to the beleaguered island nation.

The Catalina was involved in every American military action in the Pacific and a PBY crew was the first to spot the Japanese fleet in what would become known as the pivotal Battle of Midway. As the war progressed, PBYs were fitted with radar and magnetic airborne detectors, making them more efficient weapons platforms, but there was little that could be done to improve the basic airframe. When production stopped at Consolidated in March 1944 to concentrate on more modern patrol aircraft, Catalina production continued at four other plants and included the Naval Aircraft Factory PBN-1 Nomad with improved hull, uprated engines and a larger vertical tail for better stability. Boeing and Vickers built 'Cansos' for the Royal Canadian Air Force (RCAF) in Canadian factories, and even the

Above The Catalina has enjoyed an excellent career as a fire bomber in the United States, Canada, Spain and Chile. PBY-6A N6453C Tanker 85 (BuNo 64041) was originally surplused in the late 1950s and was almost immediately converted into a fire bomber, eventually becoming a *Super Cat* with the addition of two Wright R-2600 radials and cowlings from a B-25. This gave the Catalina a much needed boost in power! Following a spell in Canada as C-GFFI Tanker 9, this aircraft is still currently active as N85U. Photographed at Hemet, California, when being operated by Hemet Valley Flying Service during November 1975, N6453C still retains its side blisters, although a clipper bow has replaced the nose turret

Above right When the epic Pearl Harbor film *Tora! Tora! Tora!* was being planned in the late 1960s, a supply of Catalinas was needed for the air raid sequences. Steward-Davis of Long Beach, California, held a large store of disassembled airframes and numerous examples were put together, given a crude Navy paint scheme, and shipped to Hawaii where they were blown up for the cameras. Two of the unfortunates are seen prior to shipping at Long Beach

Right Photographed during June 1988 at Van Nuys, California, PBV-1A C-FOWE had originally been delivered to the RCAF on 5 May 1944 and was struck off charge on 7 November 1966. The aircraft became CF-OWE with Ontario Central Airlines and then passed through the hands of several other owners before being acquired by Robert Franks as N691RF. He had the aircraft rebuilt as a fabulous air yacht and took part in the dual Catalina crossing of the Atlantic in 1986 to celebrate the 75th anniversary of US Naval Aviation. However, on completion of the trip, the Catalina crashed and sank at Plymouth Harbour in England on 30 May 1986. The aircraft was raised, repaired, and flown to Canada for complete refurbishing. Currently, the Catalina is flying as N69RF out of Van Nuys

Operating a vintage aircraft off of water has to be done with skill and precision and it is not often one sees a formation water landing. With the Texan camera-ship on the edge of a stall, PYB-6A N4NC touches down gracefully, as does Grumman Albatross N226CG, flown on this occasion by Ronnie Gardner. Once on water, the amphibian dramatically slows. The distinctive tall vertical tail distinguishes the PBY-6A. N4NC retains its large side blisters, but the nose turret has been replaced with a clipper bow, which improves water handling. The PBY is flown regularly and housed in a large hangar at Big Spring, Texas, which includes several other choice warbirds owned by Wilson 'Connie' Edwards

Above Over the years, the Catalina has been modified in many ways for many uses – there was even engineering done by several firms to convert the 'Cat' to turboprop power but these plans never came to fruition. However, the most ambitious Catalina modification turned the amphibian into a four-engined aircraft with great utility, and that machine is called the bird (yes, the company makes use of a lower case 'b') *Innovator*. The *Innovator* started out life as a PBY-5A and went into RCAF service as 9746. In 1956, it was surplused as N59D and purchased by the bird Corporation of Palm Springs, California, as N5907. After several potentially disastrous powerplant failures, the company extensively re-engined the aircraft to mount two Lycoming GSO-480 engines with reversible propellers and, at the same time, extensive interior modifications were carried out. The *Innovator* is seen at Long Beach during October 1977 with its two underwing boats lowered on winches

Right Although looking a bit like a surrealist junkyard, this is actually PBY-5A N5590V (BuNo 48406) being restored back into flying condition during 1986. The owner had donated the craft to the San Diego Aerospace Museum, and a contract was issued to get it back into flying shape. This eventually happened, and N5590V flew to Naval Air Station North Island where further work was carried out. It was eventually taken to the museum and mounted on an outside plinth in August 1988 as a memorial to the many Catalinas built in San Diego. The aircraft had earlier spent many years at Van Nuys

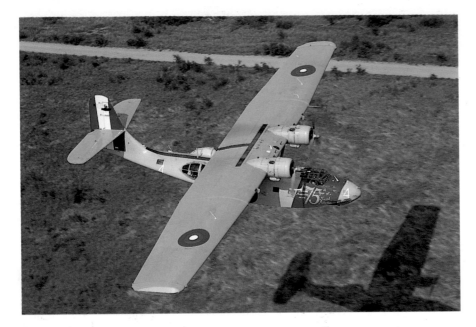

Army Air Force used the type as the OA-10 for air sea rescue. The Consolidated factory in New Orleans built PBY-5As and PBY-6As, which featured the PBN tail, increased armament, radar and other improvements. Catalina production amounted to 3281 aircraft, but the Navy was rapidly turning to the land-based patrol bomber and the days of the flying/boat amphibian were limited even though the Martin Marlin would operate with the Navy into the 1970s.

After the war, Catalinas continued to serve in frontline and reserve units (the last PBY-6A would not retire from the US Navy until 3 January 1957), but others were put into storage and sold as surplus. The Catalina found a ready market. Many were rebuilt for foreign air forces, others were converted to cargo haulers, some became deluxe 'air yachts' whilst dozens found employment as fire bombers. The type is still actively used in the latter role in both Chile and Spain, while one aircraft remained active in this capacity on the US register during 1993. Also, in 1993 the government of Quebec put its fleet of seven Catalina fire bombers up for sale, so the end of an era is rapidly approaching. However, the Catalina is a popular warbird and several examples have been restored to pristine condition and operate on the airshow circuit, where the type is certain to be a familiar sight for many years to come.

Left CF-OWE's companion on the Atlantic crossing was PBY-6A N4NC (BuNo 46662). This aircraft was surplused in the late 1950s and carried a number of different registrations including N9588C, CF-VIG, N788C, N1022G and N999AR. During 1984, the Catalina was purchased by Wilson 'Connie' Edwards of Big Spring, Texas. Edwards, a warbird collector and admirer of seaplanes, had the Catalina finished to approximate the paint scheme carried by the Curtiss NC-4s that completed the first successful Atlantic crossing. The massive wing area of the Catalina is shown to advantage as N4NC makes a high speed pass at Breckenridge, Texas, during May 1988

Right By the mid-1980s, the *Innovator* was rotting into the ground at Tico Airport in Florida and its future looked exceedingly bleak. However, veteran warbird owner Dick Durand stepped in and rescued the unique aircraft from certain extinction during 1990. Dick spent ten months pouring money into the airframe's restoration, which resulted in the finished product seen here over a fog bank near the Santa Monica Mountains on 3 October 1991 in its gleaming new paint scheme and registration N5PY. Note the clear blister on the right side of the fuselage. At this time, the two underwing 14 ft boats were not fitted. The dinghies automatically lock into position and can be used for cargo transport or water transportation. The P&W 1250 horsepower radials are augmented by the 340 hp Lycomings. N5PY is the oldest flying Catalina in the world

Consolidated Vultee Model 28 Catalina

PBY-1 to PBY-5A Catalina (data for -5)

Type: maritime patrol flying boat with normal crew of seven

Engines: two 1200 hp Pratt & Whitney R-1830-92 Twin Wasp 14-cylinder two-row radials

Dimensions: span 104 ft (31.72 m); length 63 ft 11 in (19.5 m); height 18 ft 10 in (5.65 m)

Weights: empty 17,465 lbs (7974 kg); loaded 34,000 lbs (15,436 kg)

Performance: maximum speed 196 mph (314 km/h); climb to 5000 ft (1525 m) in 4 min 30 sec; service ceiling 18,200 ft (5550 m); range at 100 mph (161 km/h) 3100 miles (4960 km)

Armament: US Navy, typically one 0.30 in or 0.50 in Browning in nose, one 0.50 in in each waist blister and one in 'tunnel' in underside behind hull step; RAF typically six 0.303 in Vickers K (sometimes Brownings) arranged one in nose, one in tunnel and pairs in blisters; wing racks for 2000 lbs (907 kg) of bombs and other stores

History: first flight (XP3Y-1) 21 March 1935; first delivery (PBY-1) October 1936; (Model 28-5 Catalina) July 1939; final delivery, after December 1945

PBY-5A N5590V was ferried into Van Nuys during 1978, and was in poor condition even at that point. It was then parked in the weeds and slowly began to return to mother nature. As can be seen, by April 1979 it had deteriorated even further, its nickname, *Tiare Tahiti*, being barely visible on the PBY's heavily weathered nose

Beech Bomber

During the late 1930s, Beech Aircraft Corporation of Wichita, Kansas, developed their Model 18 – an advanced all-metal, twin-engined low wing monoplane utilized as a light passenger or cargo aircraft. It was considerably more advanced than other contemporary aircraft. Beech staked a large portion of their future on this aircraft, but the country was still slowly recovering from the effects of the Great Depression so aircraft were not exactly pouring from the factory.

An item in a Wichita newspaper on 29 July 1938 noted a visit to the Beech factory by Lt Col Dwight Eisenhower, who was then Chief of Staff of the American military mission to the Philippine Commonwealth. Eisenhower was in Wichita to inspect a new Twin Beech purchased by the Philippine Army Air Corps and specially equipped for aerial photography. This was to the first of 5000 Model 18s which would be produced for the armed services of the Allied alliance during World War 2. Perceiving military interest in an off-the-shelf design which could be quickly adapted to specialized needs, Walter Beech ordered participation in an Air Corps evaluation competition at Wright Field in 1939. The aircraft's success in this competition resulted in the first small Air Corps contract (only 39 Twin Beeches would be produced by the start of the war).

Left Under a baking August 1942 California sun, ground crewmen load practice bombs through the entrance door of AT-11 USAAF s/n 41-9483, while aviation cadets Joseph Fleming and Mandell Cyprus look on prior to their flight from Victorville Army Air Force Base

Right Beech AT-11 N15KK is seen rumbling away from Chino Airport and heading back to its Colorado base on 12 February 1993. The AT-11 differed from the C-45 in a number of aspects, the most noticeable being the addition of the extended nose and plexiglass section, along with the small side windows in the nose. The aircraft's aluminum skin has been buffed to a high lustre, and the Kansan is finished in Army Air Corps markings. After World War 2, many AT-11s were supplied to Third World air forces by the American government

The first few C-45s ordered by the military boasted six-seat interiors and were used for transporting high ranking staff officers around the country. These aircraft were basically identical to the civilian Model 18. New orders saw rapid changes in the aircraft, and the second batch, designated C-45As and ordered in 1941, had eight-seat interiors, military avionics and other equipment, and utilised the Pratt & Whitney R-985-AN-1, which now became the standard engine for the type. All this extra equipment resulted in about a 700-pound weight increase and performance suffered. The C-45B's gross weight went up even further and speed dropped a bit more.

With the American expansion following Pearl Harbor, C-45 orders really increased with Beech receiving a contract for 1137 examples of the C-45F model. This version had the seats reduced to seven along with a few other improvements. The C-45 proved to be a real workhorse and the type's designation was changed to UC-45 at the start of 1943 to reflect the type's utility/cargo capability.

The success of the basic C-45 concept led Beech and the military to consider other uses for the design and this resulted in the AT-7, which was the military's first navigation trainer, and was fitted with chart tables and equipment for three students. The F-2 was the photographic reconnaissance version, and they were fitted with a variety of mapping cameras mounted in tandem in the cabin, with appropriate photo ports cut into the aircraft's belly. The variant illustrated in this chapter is the AT-11, which derived from the AT-7 and was utilized as a bombardier and gunnery trainer.

To accomplish this specialized mission, a number of modifications were

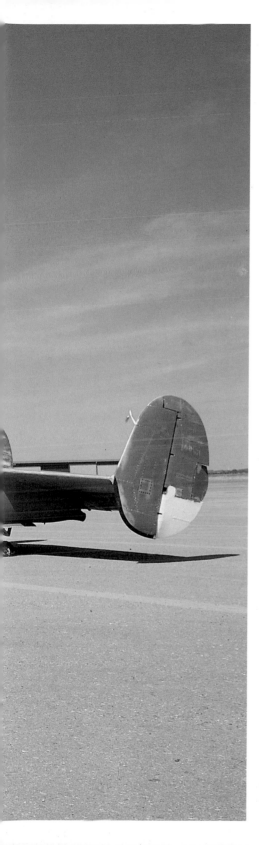

Above Kansans, after years of neglect, have achieved a very collectable status and many fine examples now fly regularly. This particular highly-polished machine has been adorned with some high class nose art

Left This Kansan was looking decidedly worse for the wear when spotted at El Paso International Airport during October 1978. With the registration N7275C crudely applied to the fuselage sides, the aircraft still wears its original markings and appears to have been flown out of a surplus yard and merely parked for years. Tyres completely flat, and several bits and pieces missing, the aircraft almost looks fit for the scrap heap

carried out to the airframe. The nose was removed immediately in front of the windshield and a large box-like section was fitted with a plexiglass nose bowl, complete with an optically perfect bomb aiming panel in the lower section. This allowed the student bombardier to wedge himself in the extreme forward fuselage where he could study his deadly art in a manner of extreme realism. The interior of the fuselage and the belly of the aircraft were also modified so that bomb racks and bomb bay doors could be fitted. Some AT-11s were built with a large bubble atop the fuselage, while many others were equipped with a powered turret for gunnery training. A small number of AT-11s were also modified to fulfil the navigational training role.

Certainly not the most glamorous of aircraft, the AT-11 was sent to training bases across the country and immediately began churning out tens of thousands of bombardiers and gunners for the nation's fleet of bombers. The C-45 (and Navy SNBs) had been given the name Expeditor but the

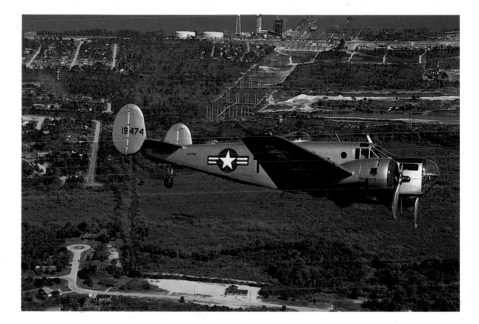

AT-11, probably due to its extensive redesign, was named Kansan. Most of
these names were mainly used for public relations for it was rare to hear a
military pilot of the time refer to an aircraft by anything more than its
designation. The AT-11 was also fitted with R-985-AN-1 radials (the AN
stood for Army, Navy) and the type performed in an efficient but seldom
publicized manner.

After the conclusion of hostilities many Twin Beeches continued to
operate with the military and AT-11s still in service after the June 1948
designation realignment were classified as T-11s. Surviving AT-11s were
sent to storage or scrap yards and the type became popular with civilian
operators who wanted mapping or survey platforms, and many of the
aircraft were transferred to the civil register. Most civil AT-11s led a hard
life, often operating in primitive conditions in remote parts of the world.
Also, some of the first fire bombers were converted AT-11s that had been
modified to drop modest amounts of borate redardant. Others were used
for the carriage of light cargo and, as the 1960s progressed, as drug runners.

By the time the warbird movement started, there were only a few of the
original 1582 AT-11s still operating. There were, however, abandoned
airframes scattered around the country and collectors began to gather these
machines and restore them, and as this book went to press, there are quite a
few very nicely restored AT-11s that can be seen on the airshow circuit.
Going from an obscure and neglected workhorse to a prized warbird, the
AT-11 now serves as a reminder of the time when America trained the
largest air force that the world has ever seen.

Above Claire Potter brings his AT-11 in close to the camera-ship. The Netherlands had ordered two dozen AT-11s, but when that country fell to the Germans, the Army took over the order and assigned the aircraft to exiled Free Dutch aviators, who had managed to escape the invasion to continue their training in the US, and this aircraft is finished in the scheme assigned to those Kansans

Right AT-11 N6586D is finished in a wildly inaccurate Air Training Command scheme and is seen during March 1983. Many AT-11s were 'upgraded' to include features found on the Model 18, and some of these can be seen on this aircraft, including the passenger windows in place of the port holes and the retractable tail wheel

Beech AT-11 Kansan

Wing Span: 47 ft 8 in
Length: 34 ft 3 in
Height: 10 ft
Wing Area: 349 sq ft
Empty Weight: 6175 lbs
Gross Weight: 8727 lbs

Max Speed: 215 mph
Rate of Climb: 10,000 ft in 10.1 min
Ceiling: 20,000 ft
Range: 750 miles

Cry Havoc

The Douglas A-20 Havoc was the most numerous of all American attack aircraft produced during World War 2 yet, today, it is one of the rarest warbird survivors. The design originally started out life during 1937 as an aircraft to sell to the growing foreign market, and during 1938 it was put into production as the DB-7 (Douglas Bomber 7) for the French *Armee de l'Air* and the Royal Air Force. Both nations needed new aircraft to counter the German threat and the DB-7 promised relatively high performance in the important attack bomber role. Under the direction of the brilliant Ed Heinemann at the company's El Segundo division, the design was originally aimed at the US Army who, in the usual manner of the time, procrastinated.

The French were eager to procure the new design and, once again in the manner of the time period, the prototype was airborne on 26 October 1938 and France rapidly placed an order for 105 machines. The initial aircraft was called the Model 7B but the French decided they wanted further modifications for the European theatre and this led to a complete rework, resulting in the DB-7. The first DB-7 flew on 17 August 1939 from Mines Field, now the site of Los Angeles International Airport and the aircraft was a success.

The Army Air Corps also liked the Douglas aircraft and, with their own modifications, ordered 206 machines, which would be designated A-20 and A-20A – both fairly direct copies of the French design. Entirely conventional in appearance and construction, the A-20 was a mid-wing aircraft with Wright R-2600 radials housed in large nacelles that also contained the main landing gear legs. The bomber featured a nose wheel which was fairly revolutionary for the time period, and although the fuselage was deep from a side profile, when viewed from the front the aircraft was quite narrow and flown by a single pilot. The A-20, 63 of which were built, was the lightest and fastest of the Havocs, as the type had been named, with a top speed of 390 mph. The early Army Havocs were used for training, as a base for conversion into F-3 photo recon platforms and as P-70 night fighters – none were used operationally in the attack role.

The French DB-7s were fitted with Pratt & Whitney R-1830-SC3G Wasps of only 900 hp each, but the aircraft was still fairly sprightly and could carry a 2000 lb bomb load. However, the first DB-7s were not used in combat until 31 May 1940, and as a result flew only a limited number of missions before the complete collapse of that nation. Surviving aircraft headed for North Africa while Britain took over the French machines still

Above A-20G USAAF s/n 43-22200 was surplused as NL63004 in 1946 and by 1952 had been converted into a six-seat executive transport. By the late 1950s, the Havoc was on a downhill slide and was repossessed by a bank and transferred to the USAF Museum in Dayton, Ohio, on 30 September 1961. The aircraft, wearing a wildly inaccurate paint scheme and still showing some of its executive modifications, is seen on display at the museum during May 1966. Since then, it has been accurately restored to its wartime appearance and is on display inside the museum's impressive new display area

on the Douglas production line. Designated the DB-7 Boston I in RAF service, the aircraft was used as a high-performance trainer, whilst those airframes delivered from the factory became Boston IIs, but these were soon transferred from Bomber to Fighter Command, where they became Havoc I night fighters fitted with early radar. Havoc IIs were inherited from the French order and were fitted with R-2600-A5B Cyclones, and these were also used for the night fighting mission.

Both Britain and America continued to order a variety of Havoc/Boston variants, and the Boston III began replacing the inadequate Bristol Blenheim light bomber. When America entered the war, many of the machines destined for the RAF were taken over for Air Corps service. Orders for 999 A-20Bs were fulfilled by opening a new Douglas factory at Long Beach, while Boeing built more DB-7Bs for the RAF under license. New variants of the Havoc came quickly as combat experience built up and more guns, bigger engines and increased armoured protection were all added. Douglas also opened up a Havoc production line at the company's original Santa Monica factory so A-20s were being rapidly delivered to America, Britain and the Soviet Union.

Left Douglas A-20G USAAF 43-21709 was purchased as one of several hundred surplus aircraft snapped up by the ever enterprising Paul Mantz on 19 February 1946 from a War Assets storage yard in Oklahoma. Mantz drained the fuel from the tanks of the various aircraft, sold it for enough money to cover the purchase, and then parted with the majority of the airframes for a profit as scrap. Originally registered as NC67932, Mantz soon sold the A-20, and somewhere along the line it received an executive interior. As the years went by, the aircraft steadily deteriorated until it was finally purchased as a hulk by William Farah of El Paso, Texas, during 1970. Farah started an extensive restoration campaign and brought the aircraft, now registered N3WF, back to life. It was photographed during October 1979 on a sortie from its nearby El Paso base, and as can be seen, even though the Havoc was a later G-model, it was finished in an early Air Corps scheme. On 16 September 1991, the Havoc was sold to the Lone Star Flight Museum in Galveston, Texas

America staged its first Havoc raid on Occupied Europe on 4 July 1942 with mixed results, the USAAF squadrons having to make up the numbers with borrowed RAF machines. A-20s were also at Pearl Harbor for the 7 December 1941 raid, but most were destroyed or damaged on the ground. Since the Havoc was being rapidly churned out in large numbers, it was not long before the aircraft was in action on most Allied combat fronts. Many Havocs were modified in the field to carry more weapons and armour, and additional nose guns made it a very effective low-level strafer. Another main variant was the A-20G which had (for the first 250 produced) four 20 mm and two .50 calibre nose guns. Douglas built a further 2600 Gs and these were fitted with six .50 calibre guns in the nose, while the majority also had an upper Martin power turret with two similar weapons. A .50 calibre on a swivel mount was also fitted in the belly.

The A-20J was similar to the G-model, but had a glass bombardier's nose and two .50 calibre nose guns. The A-20H and A-20K were powered with R-2600-20s of 1700 hp each, and the H-model had the six .50 calibre gun nose while the K had the glass unit. The Havoc fought long and hard, although it was not a glamorous aircraft and failed to receive much publicity. Douglas had built 7098 aircraft by the time production ended on 20 September 1944, and Boeing added another 380 aircraft to the overall total. At its peak, seven USAAF groups flew the Havoc. In Europe, the aircraft normally functioned as a medium altitude bomber, but in the Pacific, the Havocs came in at palm tree height for lightning strikes against the Japanese. The Soviets benefited from Lend-Lease and were assigned a total of 3125 Havocs, of which 2908 were eventually handed over.

By the conclusion of the war, the USAAF had little use for the A-20 and many were simply blown up at foreign fields while those in the United States were assigned to storage yards and put up for surplus sale by War Assets. The Havoc found few civilian buyers, but the handful that did escape the scrapper's torch were converted to executive transports, although the very narrow fuselage did not really lend itself to conversion. The ever-eccentric Howard Hughes was drawn to the A-20 and purchased a couple, having at least one converted to executive standards. By the mid-1960s, the majority of the survivors had simply disappeared, and the sole remaining Hughes aircraft, N34920, sat for years in a tightly guarded compound at Hughes Airport in Culver City. William Farah rescued a very derelict A-20G in 1970 and spent years bringing the aircraft back to flying condition. The Confederate Air Force (CAF) also rescued a worn-out A-20G that had been an executive aircraft for Hearst Magazines before becoming a crop sprayer. In poor condition, the CAF managed to fly the warbird out of Boise, Idaho, in 1966, and then spent years restoring the aircraft only to have an 'over age' pilot suffer a heart attack whilst flying it at the CAF's 1988 airshow in front of a sell-out crowd. The aircraft was totally destroyed in the ensuing crash.

Above A-20G USAAF s/n 43-22210 was purchased by Hearst Magazines Inc and converted into an executive transport during 1946 as NL67921. By 1950, Hearst had sold the Havoc and it went through several owners until being obtained by the Roberts Aircraft Co, who modified it into a large acreage sprayer. By the early 1960s, the bomber was derelict and parked in the weeds at Boise, Idaho. At this point, the growing CAF stepped in and purchased the Havoc on 5 October 1965, immediately despatching a team of mechanics to the aircraft to restore it back into flying shape for the ferry flight from Boise to Harlingen, Texas, which was duly undertaken on 12 September 1966. Once at the CAF base, work on the A-20 proceeded at a steady rate until the aircraft finally emerged in an inaccurate paint scheme in 1976 as, at the time, the only flying example of the Havoc. As can be seen, the executive modifications such as windows and modified nose are still present. Unfortunately, under the CAF policy of 'pay and fly', an elderly pilot, who held a current FAA medical license and who had invested heavily in the aircraft, flew the bomber during the organisation's annual event in 1988 . Whilst performing his routine, the pilot suffered a massive heart attack and the Havoc rolled over and pitched into the ground, with fatal results for both the pilot and the aircraft

Right David Tallichet recovered an abandoned A-20 from Nicaragua where it had been on display in a Managua park. This aircraft had been registered as N5066N to the Delta Drilling Co in 1947, and the Havoc passed through the hands of several owners before being converted into an executive transport in the early 1950s. At some point, it was acquired by Nicaragua and presumably used as a transport (perhaps the 'Air Force One' of Nicaragua), where it carried the serial FAN 50. Tallichet, in-between the political and military battles wracking the unstable nation, managed to recover the aircraft between 1975 and 1977 and then stored it at Chino. During 1991, Tallichet worked out a lease agreement with Air Heritage Inc of Beaver Falls, Pennsylvania, and the airframe was trucked to the new location from Chino. Air Heritage hopes to completely restore the Havoc, which has now been registered N99385, back to its original military condition. Judging by the state of the airframe, this will be both a time consuming and expensive task. The close-up view focuses on the faded Nicaraguan national insignia which adorns the fuselage of the A-20H

Currently, the only flying Havoc is the ex-Farah A-20G which was purchased by the Lone Star Flight Museum in Galveston, Texas, and as of August 1993, the group were debating on whether to keep the aircraft permanently grounded because of its rarity. Kermit Weeks has obtained the ex-Hughes machine, which is in poor condition and currently stored in the California desert, but he hopes to have the aircraft made flyable in the future. David Tallichet recovered several Havocs from diverse locations during the 1970s, one of these aircraft, A-20H N99385, having since been leased to Air Heritage Inc of Beaver Falls, Pennsylvania, where it is under long-term restoration back to flying status. Another former executive conversion, A-20H N63004, is on display at the USAF Museum at Wright-Patterson AFB, Ohio. With very few surviving examples in existance across the globe today, the A-20 has now become one of the most ultra-exotic of all American *Bombing Twins*.

Douglas DB-7 family

A-20, Boston, Havoc, BD-2, F-3 and P-70
Type: two-seat fighter and intruder, three-seat bomber or two-seat reconnaissance aircraft
Engines: early DB-7 versions (Boston I, II, Havoc II) two 1200 hp Pratt & Whitney R-1830-S3C4-G Twin Wasp 14-cylinder two-row radials; all later versions, two 1500, 1600 or 1700 hp Wright GR-2600-A5B, -11, -23 or -29 Double Cyclone 14-cylinder two-row radials
Dimensions: span 61 ft 4 in (18.69 m); length varied from 45 ft 11 in to 48 ft 10 in (A-20G, 48 ft 4 in, 14.74 m); height 17 ft 7 in (5.36 m)
Weights: early Boston/Havoc, typically empty 11,400 lbs (5171 kg), loaded 16,700 lbs (7574 kg); (A-20G, typical of main production); empty 12,950 lbs (5874 kg), loaded 27,200 lbs (12,340 kg)
Performance: maximum speed, slowest early versions 295 mph (475 km/h); fastest versions 351 mph (565 km/h); (A-20G) 342 mph (549 km/h); initial climb 1200-2000 ft (366-610 m) min; service ceiling typically 25,300 ft (7720 m); range with maximum weapon load typically 1000 miles (1610 km)

Armament: (Havoc 1), eight 0.303 in Brownings in nose, one 0.303 in Vickers K manually aimed in rear cockpit; (Havoc II) twelve 0.303 in in nose, (Havoc intruder), four 0.303 in in nose, one Vickers K, and 1000 lb (454 kg) Bomb load: (A-20B) two fixed 0.5 in Brownings on sides of nose, one 0.5 in manually aimed dorsal, one 0.30 in manually aimed ventral, 200 lb (907 kg) bomb load; (Boston III bomber) four fixed 0.303 in one sides of nose, twin manually aimed 0.303 in dorsal, twin manually aimed 0.303 in ventral, 2000 lb (907 kg) bomb load: (Boston III intruder) belly tray of four 20 mm Hispano cannon, 2000 lb (907 kg) bomb load; (A-20G) four 20 mm and two 0.5 in or six 0.5 in in nose, dorsal turret with two 0.5 in, manually aimed 0.5 in ventral, 4000 lb (1814 kg) bomb load. Many other schemes, early A-20s having fixed rearward firing 0.30 in in each nacelle
History: first flight (Douglas 7B) 26 October 1938; (production DB-7) 17 August 1939; service delivery (France) 2 January 1940; termination of production September 1944

Mitchell Magnificence

To the casual aviation observer, the shape of the North American B-25 Mitchell medium bomber is one of familiarity. Although born in the decade to which the term 'streamline' has been freely applied by historians, the Mitchell's distinctive blunt lines, large cowled engines and trademark twin vertical tails bear the stamp of workman utilitarianism rather than a form of effete stylization. From the very start, the Mitchell was built to be a practical machine with only one purpose – the art of war.

The fledgling North American Aviation Company had left the small factory at Dundalk, Maryland, where several designs, including the O-47 Army general purpose observation craft, had been instigated and constructed in small numbers. Under the presidency of James H 'Dutch' Kindelberger, who was ably supported by chief engineer John Leland Atwood, the company's assets transferred to Inglewood in southern

15-gun salute from American flyers

North American Aviation Sets the Pace

Left *Desert Warrior* racked up 73 combat missions before being flown back to the States from North Africa. The aircraft was flown by a crew made up of the four squadrons comprising the 12th Bomb Group, 'The Earthquakers'. The Mitchell was utilized for a war bond drive

Where there's a fight there's a Mitchell

North American Aviation *Sets the Pace!*

MITCHELL BOMBERS SMASH JAP BASE AT RABAUL

NORTH AMERICAN *Sets the Pace!*

California where rent was cheap and the weather benign. A new factory, claimed to be the first constructed to build modern aircraft, was set up on what is now the site of Los Angeles International Airport.

Starting out with 150 employees in a 159,000 square foot building, North American went to work on a new trainer design – the NA-16 (which would later, after numerous variants, metamorphose into the immortal AT-6 Texan) – while completing the O-47 contract. By this time, (January 1936), southern California had become the hotbed of aviation with companies like Douglas, Lockheed, Vultee and Northrop building a variety of new designs, many of which would revolutionize air travel and air combat.

In a not unwise move, Kindelberger decided to concentrate on the military market and leave the civil aircraft field to other concerns. Tension in the far east and Europe began to result in aircraft orders that had been undreamed of by American aeronautical concerns. Suddenly, it seemed that every non-Axis nation needed military aircraft of every type in order to build up their air forces to counter the growing military threat of international fascism.

During 1938, the Army Air Corps circulated a proposal for the development of a new twin-engine attack bomber in a document titled Circular Proposal 38-385. The North American response was the NA-40, designed by Atwood and Raymond Rice. The NA-40 was powered by two Pratt & Whitney R-1830 radials, had twin vertical tails, a crew of three, and could carry a rather minuscule bomb load of 1200 lbs. First flying in January 1939, the aircraft was soon modified with more powerful engines and other improvements. Sent to Wright Field (the Edwards AFB of its day), the sole NA-40 was destroyed in a pilot induced accident and the lucrative contract went to Douglas and their design, which would become the A-20 Havoc.

With the NA-40, which was fitted with 'modern' tricycle landing gear, North American had gained experience that proved beneficial when the Air Corps asked the company to expand on the design. The new aircraft was given the company designation of NA-62, and the design so impressed the Air Corps that it was ordered right off the drawing board in September 1939 with a 186-airframe contract worth $11.7 million. North American was now truly established.

To give an idea of the rapidity of work and urgency of the time, the first NA-62 prototype (now given the Air Corps designation B-25 and the name Mitchell for America's main proponent of aerial bombardment, Billy Mitchell) took to the air on 19 August 1940. The B-25 did not look unlike the NA-40. The distinctive twin vertical tails were back, as well as the tricycle landing gear, but the wing was now mounted mid-fuselage rather than on the shoulder, and the fuselage had been widened so that the pilot and co-pilot would sit side-by-side rather than in tandem. Two Wright

Above Stephens County Airport, Breckenridge, Texas, is the home to a fine collection of warbirds including TB-25N USAAF serial number 44-30456 N43BA, owned and flown by former World War 2 pilot William G Arnot. Seen on a June 1991 outing near its Breckenridge home, the Mitchell is named *Silver Lady* and is maintained in immaculate condition and kept in its own custom hangar. S/n 44-30456 started out in civilian life in 1962 as N3512G but the aircraft was not widely used and eventually lapsed into dereliction at Galveston, where it was obtained by Bob Diemert of Canada, who got the machine back into flying shape in 1973 as C-GTTS. Bill Arnot obtained the B-25 in 1982, and had the aircraft rebuilt back into pristine condition. N43BA has been fitted with a custom-built container that fits into the bomb bay and is raised and lowered by a winch. Spare parts and luggage can be carried in the container, which is a most useful addition when visiting distant airshows

Right The twin vertical tails of the Mitchell make the aircraft the most identifiable of all medium bombers. As the value of these veterans increased during the 1970s and 80s, it made sense for the owners to lavish time and money on their investments. This close-up view of N43BA illustrates the immaculate condition in which the aircraft is kept

Right One of the first individuals to recognize the historic value of surplus wartime aircraft was Ed Maloney who established The Air Museum in the early 1950s. Maloney was able to gather together many airframes that were simply being tossed out by the military or by technical schools. However, keeping such a collection intact was not an easy task. Originally operating a small museum near Cable-Claremont Airport in southern California, Maloney moved to much large facilities at Ontario Airport. When that airport began expanding, Maloney was forced to move again, eventually settling at Chino Airport, where the museum would become an attraction for every aviation enthusiast. Between moves, many aircraft had to be stored in a vacant lot near Ontario Airport, where they were at the mercy of the elements and vandals. B-25J USAAF s/n 44-30761 is seen in less than ideal condition in the storage yard, its paint peeling, plexiglass smashed and many parts removed. The Mitchell was on loan to the museum from the USAF when photographed during June 1974. Since the aircraft was in poor condition, it was taken back under USAF control and offered to other organizations. When no interested party came forth, the Mitchell was scrapped

R-2600-7 radials of 1700 horsepower each were fitted and, since the aircraft was coming right off the drawing board, numerous changes were made including the modification of the outer wing panels to have a rather gull-winged appearance rather than straight line dihedral from wing root to tip that distinguished the first nine B-25s.

Aircraft flowed from the production line in a series of constantly improving models that would remain in production until the end of World War 2, a total of 9889 Mitchells being built – more than any other American medium bomber. The B-25 was the first multi-engined combat aircraft from North American to achieve series production, and advertisements in the aviation periodicals of the time made extensive note of that fact. The Mitchell was rushed into Air Corps service and the first unit to operate the type was the 17th Bombardment Group (Medium), who went on to destroy the first Japanese submarine in the Pacific on 24 December 1941 (this excludes the Japanese 'midget' subs which were destroyed in the attack on Pearl Harbor).

As improvements and modifications were introduced on the production line, new variants rapidly began to appear. For example, the B-25B included both dorsal and ventral electrically operated Bendix turrets. The ventral turret was completely retractable and the gunner used a periscope to sight his weapons. These early variants were built in fairly small batches and only 120 B-models were completed before the line was once again changed.

Left When Maloney established The Air Museum at Chino, many of the stored aircraft were transferred to the new facility, which expanded over the years to become one of the top veteran and vintage aircraft museums. B-25J USAAF s/n 44-30423 N3675G was owned by the museum and moved to Chino where, after considerable work, it became one of the most flown aircraft in the collection. The machine became widely in demand as a camera platform for films, television and commercials as the Tallmantz Mitchell operation became less active. Photographed on 20 March 1993, N3675G is seen in its most recent scheme, appropriately named Photo Fanny, and being flown by Kevin Eldridge, near the Mitchell's Chino base. The aircraft had its usual olive drab paint stripped off and the aluminum skin polished for a starring (as well as working) role in the Mel Gibson film *Forever Young*. Not only did it appear in the film, the B-25 also served as a camera platform. The interior of N3398G has been optimized for aerial camera work and is fitted with a 'director's chair' with video monitors. Note the bubble that has replaced the turret, and which serves as a useful observation station during filming. The .50 calibre package guns on the side of the fuselage are also very evident. Visibility from the multi-framed canopy is not the best, and pilot Eldridge can be seen leaning forward to keep the camera ship in sight

Above For many years, The Air Museum owned a second flyable Mitchell. This aircraft was the historic VB-25J USAAF s/n 43-4030, which had been extensively modified as the personal transport for Gen Dwight D Eisenhower, Supreme Commander of Allied Forces during World War 2. This aircraft was built at the Kansas City plant but flown to Inglewood in February 1944 for modifications. The aircraft was stripped of all surplus equipment and the waist gun positions were removed and skinned over while a series of windows was added on each side of the fuselage. The cockpit canopy was also modified and the interior was soundproofed. A bunk bed, chairs and sofa were installed, and the bomb bay was lowered to provide better access to the cockpit area. A custom long-range bullet-proof fuel tank was also fitted in place of ordnance in the compact bomb bay. The tail gun position was removed and a life raft was installed in the vacant position, which could be automatically jettisoned in the event of a water landing. The aircraft was delivered to Britain during May 1944, and Eisenhower apparently used the transport for at least one flight over the planned Allied landing beaches for the upcoming D-Day invasion on 6 June. After the war, the Mitchell operated with several VIP USAF transport groups, and its last assignment was with the 1001st Air Base Wing at Andrews AFB in 1958. The VB-25J was struck from the USAF inventory in February 1959 and stored at Davis-Monthan AFB in Arizona until sold as surplus as N3339G. It passed through the hands of several civilian owners until being acquired by The Air Museum in the 1960s. The Mitchell is seen at Long Beach Airport during March 1979 when it was being used in film work. In 1984, the machine was transferred to the USAF Museum, and it is currently on display at Ellsworth AFB in South Dakota

Above Surplus Mitchells that were not immediately put to work were often left to merely sit around in the weeds until some money-making use could be found for the former bombers. In the early 1960s it was not uncommon to find semi-abandoned Mitchells at diverse locations across the USA. Unfortunately, as the 1960s progressed, many of these aircraft were scrapped. One Mitchell that did survive was B-25J USAAF s/n 45-8884, which was surplused as N3156G and saw little in the way of flying. The aircraft was purchased by Johan M Larsen of Minneapolis, Minnesota, during the late 1960s for his Minnesota Aircraft Museum. Larsen was instrumental in saving several aircraft that probably would have been scrapped during this time period, including a rare North American O-47. During 1979, N3156G was purchased by Canadian Warbird collector Jerry Janes, and the aircraft was made flyable and ferried to Chino Airport for further restoration work. Despite years of outside storage, the B-25 was in surprisingly good condition and is seen during March 1979 as work on the airframe progressed

Left Jerry Janes originally had N3156G finished in period USAAF markings with the name *Death Watch*. Janes is seen piloting his P-51D Mustang while the bomber flies wing during October 1979

Although the Mitchell fought throughout America's participation in World War 2, the type's true moment of lasting fame came on 18 April 1942 when 16 B-25Bs under the command of Lt Col James H 'Jimmy' Doolittle launched off the deck of the USS *Hornet* while 800 miles from the coast of Japan. This daring and highly-classified raid saw Army bombers operating from a Navy carrier for the first time, and the rather arrogant enemy was caught completely by surprise in America's morale-boosting first strike on Japan. Damage done by the raid was minimal, and all the Mitchells were lost. However, the effects on the home front were tremendous and the Doolittle Raid became the hallmark of America's long fight to regain control of the Pacific. Lessons learned in combat over Europe were quickly incorporated into the B-25 production line, and more armour and defensive weapons were added. The Mitchell, and its stablemate the B-26 Marauder, began to replace obsolete Douglas B-18 Bolos and B-23 Dragons, while orders began to build up from the Army as well as from Lend-Lease Allies. With the B-25C, Mitchell tempo increased as the contract for this version covered a whopping 863 aircraft to be completed at the Inglewood factory

Above By 1982, Janes had changed the registration of N3156G to C-GCWJ and the airframe was finished in postwar RCAF No 418 'City of Edmonton' Sqn markings, complete with 'Arctic red' panels in case the Mitchell force-landed in snow. The RCAF obtained 75 B-25Js in 1951 to augment the survivors of an original 70 Mitchell Mk IIIs received during the war; the RCAF finally phased out its last Mitchell in 1963. As this book went to press, '884 is registered N5833B and owned by Randall Porter of Woodstock, Georgia

Above One of the most impressive collections of airworthy warbirds around today is that operated by the Lone Star Flight Museum in Galveston. During the late 1980s and early 1990s, Lone Star added many aircraft to its fleet and opened a world class operational flying museum in historic Galveston. One of the first aircraft purchased by Lone Star was B-25J USAAF s/n 44-86734 N333RW, which today is finished as a very glossy US Navy PBJ-1J – both the Navy and Marines flew the Mitchell in large numbers during World War 2. All of Lone Star's aircraft are very highly detailed, with many parts being polished, chromed or anodized. Mitchells were fitted with a wide variety of .50 calibre nose guns during the war, and N333RW sports two of the weapons mounted on the extreme right side of the bombardier's position, along with the four package guns on the sides of the fuselage. The Special Delivery nose art which adorns the aircraft recreates one of Alberto Vargas' most famous 'pin-up' paintings. Originally surplused in 1961, this Mitchell was given the civil registration N9090Z and went through several owners before becoming derelict. It was acquired and made airworthy by Dean Martin in 1979 as N600DM and sold to Lone Star shortly after. Seen here gracefully departing Breckenridge, *Special Delivery* has been left devoid of the top turret on economic grounds as it flies many trips away from Texas throughout the year and the crew appreciate the extra speed. The author can testify that a Mitchell trip across America will try even the hardiest of souls, to say nothing of destroying one's hearing

which, even with expansion, was being stretched to the seams with the demand for T-6s and P-51s.

In order to keep combat aircraft flowing to the various theatres of war, a new factory was constructed in Kansas City which began producing the first of 1200 B-25Ds, an aircraft identical to the B-25C. As more groups trained on the Mitchell, the type began to spread across the globe in the battle against the Axis, and some remarkable early successes were scored against the Japanese in the south-west Pacific, where the rugged bomber proved very effective in low altitude raids against enemy shipping and airfields.

Many B-25s were modified in the field to carry extra machine guns, armour and bombs, and word of these modifications got back to North American who incorporated some in the next batch of production aircraft. One of the most interesting modifications saw the fitting of a 75 mm cannon in the nose of the XB-25G. This very heavy punch could easily sink lightly armoured Japanese shipping, and soon after tests proved that the mod would work 400 B-25Gs were sent to the fighting. The B-25H was also fitted with the 75 mm cannon in the nose, but it also had four .50 calibre

Above As previously mentioned, many Mitchells were chopped up for scrap during the 1960s, this very mangled and unidentified example being picked apart at Merrill Field, Anchorage, Alaska, on 11 May 1973. Quite a few Mitchells made Alaska their home, the type finding employment as a fire bomber and as a cargo and fish hauler

Right The Mitchell made a useful fire bomber (the first example being created in the 1950s by famed Hollywood stunt pilot Paul Mantz) until several inflight structural failures saw the type withdrawn from service in the United States. TB-25N USAAF s/n 44-28938 was surplused in the early 1960s with the civil registration N7946C. The aircraft was converted as a fire bomber and operated by Wenatchee Air Service in Washington before going to Red Dodge Aviation in Anchorage where it continued its fire bombing career starting in the late 1960s (Red Dodge used a pink P-51D as a spotter aircraft for his fire bombers). N7946C is seen at Anchorage on 11 May 1973 after it had been withdrawn from operations. In the late 1970s, the Mitchell headed south to California where it was acquired by Jim Ricketts' Aero Nostalgia in 1982. The large nose art features Snoopy saying 'Happiness is a thunderstorm'. Note the odd drooped wing tips on Tanker 4

Browning air cooled machine guns for added punch, as well as being capable of carrying 3200 lbs of bombs. The Army ordered 1000 B-25IIs, and later models were fitted with up to 14 .50 calibre machine guns, an armament fit that could effectively deal with just about anything the Japanese operated in the air, on land or at sea. By July 1944, the North American Inglewood factory had ceased Mitchell production, switching over to Mustangs.

The most numerous Mitchell variant was the B-25J, and North American built 4318 starting in April 1943. The J-model was delivered with a glass bombardier's nose, and many sub-variants were built including the J-22, which had 12 .50 calibre machine guns installed with 7300 rounds of ammunition for the weapons. Combined with its bomb load, the B-25J was a formidable weapon. A typical ordnance package could comprise two 1600 lb bombs, three 1000 lb bombs or six 500 lb bombs, and a Mk 13 torpedo could be fitted externally. Along with the USAAF, the Mitchell was widely used by the Navy and Marines as the PBJ-1. Other Allied nations that utilized the medium bomber included the Soviet Union, Britain, The Netherlands and Australia

Mitchell production came to an end in August 1945 with the atomic bombing of Japan. North American had delivered 9816 Mitchells, but the war's end saw 72 J-35s completed but not delivered. These aircraft were flown to storage or scrap yards and incomplete Mitchells on the production line were simply chopped up and sold off by the pound to the scrap man.

Above When Jim Ricketts got N7946C to his Aero Nostalgia facility at Stockton, California, he set out to create the finest restored Mitchell on the airshow circuit. He stripped out all the fire bomber gear and began a search to find original internal Mitchell equipment. He also gave the aircraft's aluminum skin extreme attention with the buffing wheel, and when the aircraft was displayed at the August 1982 Madera Gathering of Warbirds, the Mitchell literally glowed from all the attention that Jim had lavished upon it – the aircraft was not recognizable as the former 'working girl' Tanker 4. The elaborate Dream Lover nose art and all the original interior equipment, including a working upper turret, had created an award winner, but just a month later while on a flight to the Reno Air Races, the pilot in command overflew Stead Airport, where the event was being held, and found himself lost. The aircraft ran out of gas and made a gear down landing in the desert. The nose gear buckled and the glass bombardier nose was torn off. A rescue team went out to the accident site, put the nose gear down, and towed the craft back to Stead. A spare nose was fitted to the B-25, along with new props and it was flown back to Stockton where it remains in a hangar to this day

Above B-25J USAAF s/n 44-31508 was registered as N6578D in 1963 and went through several owners in the Miami area before being acquired by Euramerica Air Inc in 1966 for use in a projected movie about the Battle of Britain. The aircraft was heavily modified into a camera configuration and painted in a variety of brilliant dayglo colours for visibility (and, in best 1960s' tradition, given the name *Psychedelic Monster*). The aircraft was flown across the Atlantic and extensively utilized in the film, which gestated into reality as *Battle of Britain*. Filming continued through 1967 and 1968 and, when finished, there was little further work in Britain for the highly modified bomber. It once again flew across the Atlantic and firmly planted itself at Caldwell-Wright Field in New

Jersey, where it began to return to Mother Nature as a vandalized hulk. The ruin was purchased by Tom Reilly, who spent months camped beside the Mitchell as he restored the craft back to airworthiness in preparation for a long ferry flight back to his hangar at Kissimmee, Florida. Once safely 'down south', the aircraft was fully refurbished as the first of many B-25s to pass through Reilly's 'Bomber Town' in the 1980s – he also restored the fabulous Collings Foundation's Consolidated B-24J Liberator to airworthy status. In 1983, N6578D was sold to the B-25 Bomber Group and based at Titusville, Florida. The aircraft is appropriately named *Chapter XI* for nothing can drain a bank account more quickly than a vintage bomber!

The end of the war did not mean an end to Mitchell operations, however. Many aircraft were flown back to the US from combat zones, while others were simply destroyed and scrapped at their bases. Storage yards across the country were full of surplus military aircraft and the War Assets Administration was formed to dispose of this huge inventory. Most aircraft were offered for sale either in flyable condition or as scrap. Many returning pilots now in civilian life wanted nothing to do with aircraft ever again, while others were eager to pick up an inexpensive machine to pursue their flying careers. Many Mitchells earnt new employment as they were desired for use as work aircraft since the airframe could be easily modified to perform a number of roles such as cargo or passenger hauling. North American even saw the potential of converting Mitchell airframes into highly-modified executive aircraft, but this programme came to an end when the prototype came apart in a thunderstorm, killing seven NAA officials.

The Mitchell was retained in some numbers by the new US Air Force (created in 1947) as crew and radar trainers. Between 1950 and 1954, many Mitchells were modified into TB-25J trainers (over 600 modified after the war), TB-25K fire control trainers (117 Js modified by Hughes Aircraft in 1951), TB-25L pilot trainers (90 Js modified by Hayes Aircraft), TB-25M fire control radar trainers (40 Js modified by Hughes in 1952) and TB-25N pilot trainers (47 Js modified by Hayes in 1954). These upgraded and completely rebuilt Mitchells soldiered on with the USAF until the last examples were retired in the early 1960s.

Left Paul Mantz, who later combined forces with Frank Tallman to create Tallmantz Aviation at Orange County Airport in southern California, was an early user of the B-25. Mantz undertook the first fire bomber conversion of a Mitchell and then went on to heavily modify two B-25s into aerial camera platforms. The first Mitchell so modified was TB-25H USAAF s/n 43-4643 N1203 *The Bug Smasher*, which shot sequences for dozens of films and co-starred in Catch 22, with its owner at the controls. Mantz acquired the aircraft from War Assets at Seacy Field, Oklahoma, on 19 February 1946 and kept it until 1978 when Tallmantz unwittingly sold the historic Mitchell to a Van Nuys drug dealer, who promptly crashed the B-25 on a 'run' into Columbia. The second Tallmantz photo Mitchell was VB-25N USAAF s/n 44-30823. Assigned the civil registration N1042 in 1958, this aircraft went through various owners until arriving at Tallmantz in 1962. Photographed at Orange County (note all the other Tallmantz rarities in the background) during January 1969, the Mitchell is finished in Tallmantz house colours and displays the flags of all the nations over which the aircraft operated. The panoramic camera nose even features curtains! This aircraft was sold in 1985 and is now based with Aces High at the former Battle of Britain airfield of North Weald. It was used extensively during the filming of the B-17 epic *Memphis Belle* in 1989, and is still kept in flyable condition today

Above TB-25N USAAF s/n 44-30606 N201L was
surplused in 1963, the Mitchell being registered as
N5249V and going on to become one of the few civilian
B-25s to be modified into a corporate transport with an
airstair door, extra windows and an executive interior. In
1989, N201L was purchased by Ted Melsheimer of Carson
City, Nevada. Rather than go to the great expense of
modifying the B-25 back to stock condition, Ted decided
to have Aero Trader go through the airframe and repair

any faults, while adding a top turret, replica machine
guns and other bits of military equipment. Thus, the
owner could have a warbird with a comfortable interior.
N201L was given some elaborate nose art and the name
Tootsie, and is now flown regularly by Melsheimer and his
crew, who keep it in excellent condition in its Carson City
hangar. In this view, N201L is accompanied by a later
North American product, a T-28B Trojan

Right Given the fact that barely one percent of the entire Mitchell production run still survives, it is amazing that B-25 USAAC s/n 40-2168 is still with us. This aircraft was the fourth Mitchell built, and was chosen for conversion into a VIP transport for Gen Hap Arnold in 1943. The aircraft was completed at the Inglewood factory in July 1943 and, with its 'executive' interior, was assigned to Arnold soon after. The B-25 was not over used, and when it was declared surplus to requirements in July 1945, the airframe had amassed only 300 hours of flying time. Sold by War Assets, the aircaft was given the registration N75831. The aircraft was used by a Chicago bank for cross-country trips, and while tied down at the Hughes Airport in Culver City, California, the transport Mitchell caught the eye of the field's namesake. Howard had a strange predilection for bombers converted to transports and owned several B-23 Dragons and A-20 Havocs so modified. He offered the bank a deal it could not refuse, and became owner of the B-25 on 28 June 1951. It remained in Hughes' ownership until 1962, apparently rarely flown. When sold, some sources state it was assigned the Mexican registration XB-GOG. The B-25 resurfaced once again in 1967 and became N2825B, passing through several owners until purchased by Dewey Miller of Mobile, Alabama, on 28 August 1977. By this time, the aircraft was getting rather tired and had been subjected to considerable abuse, including five years as an outdoor exhibit at the now defunct SST Aviation Museum in Kissimmee, Florida. Miller recognized the historic importance of his aircraft and put lots of money and work into getting the rare B-25 back into good condition. Named *Proud Mary* after Dewey's wife, N2825B is seen with gear and flaps down, heading in for landing at Madera, California, during August 1983. When redoing the B-25, Dewey added Arnold's rank insignia and the short-lived 1943 red surround to the 'stars and bars' – just the way it was when NAA delivered the aircraft to the general. Additional windows, lack of a bomb bay and the custom-built nose are all clearly visible. Miller sold the transport in 1983, and the craft went through several owners until purchased by Jeff Clyman, owner of the Cockpit series of stores, in 1989. Considerable corrosion was discovered in the airframe but this was repaired by Aero Trader. However, the unique transport nose gave way to a bombardier glass unit. The aircraft is often seen on the east coast airshow circuit

Throughout the 1950s and into the early 1960s, Mitchell surplus sales continued and some of the civilian aircraft were modified into fire bombing or photo mapping platforms. By the mid-1960s, most of the Mitchell fleet was put out to pasture, but the film *Catch 22* saw 18 bombers gathered from across the country and put into airworthy condition for motion picture work. Employment by the Paramount studio saved many Mitchells from the junkyard, and the start of the warbird movement in the late 1960s began to see Mitchells restored back to their original military condition. Today, the B-25 is the most numerous of the surviving 'Bombing Twins'.

Above B-25J USAAF s/n 44-86724 CF-NTU was one of at least four ex-CAF Mitchells derelict at Kamloops, British Columbia, during August 1977. Stripped of its engines and other vital parts, CF-NTU was delivered to the RCAF as 5203 on 6 July 1951 and dropped from service on 26 April 1962. Along with the other Mitchells, CF-NTU was ferried to Kamloops, where the aircraft was probably going to be converted to perform either cargo hauling or fire bombing. At this point in time, all the Mitchells at Kamloops looked pretty bad but CF-NTU was the worst. However, while it appears that the other B-25s were probably scrapped, CF-NTU is still with us, the airframe being obtained by the CAF and restored back to static condition. Today it proudly guards the gate at CAFB Winnipeg, Manitoba, as a reminder of a not so distant past when the prairie reverberated to the thunder of the mighty Wrights

Above right Another rare Mitchell survivor is RB-25D USAAF s/n 43-3634 N3774. One of only four known surviving D-models, this aircraft was assigned to the RCAF as Mitchell II KL148 on 18 October 1944 and enjoyed a long life with the force before finally being put up for disposal on 18 June 1962. The aircraft found a ready buyer in Ontario, where it was registered CF-NWV. In 1966, it was

purchased by Glenn Lamont of Detroit, Michigan, who kept the craft in flying condition until he sold N3774 to the Yankee Air Force Museum in Ypsilanti, Michigan. From fairly humble beginnings, the Yankee Air Force Museum has built up an imposing force of aircraft including a B-17G that is nearing restoration back to flying status as this book goes to press. With flaps down, N3774 is seen rolling in for a pass over the grass runway at the National Warplane Museum's annual airshow at Geneseo on 16 August 1992. The B-25D carries the name *Yankee Warrior*, along with appropriate nose art. Oddly, the bomber is finished in a postwar scheme, complete with a heat-dissipating white top. Note the replica machine guns added to the nose

Right Nose held high for maximum aerodynamic breaking, Wiley Sanders brings *Georgia Mae* in for a landing at Breckenridge. *Georgia Mae* is TB-25N USAAF s/n 44-86785 N5262V, and was originally purchased surplus by Charles 'Red' Jensen, a colourful crop duster/fire bomber pilot, in 1958 and then kept in storage in a hangar at Tonopah, Nevada, until being sold in 1978. Sanders acquired the aircraft in 1983 and has improved its condition over the years, fitting an operational upper turret along with much original equipment for the interior

Above *Ol Gray Mare* engages in some tail chasing with *Georgia Mae*. Wearing a very distinctive paint scheme that we are fairly sure was never applied to any Mitchell, *Ol Gray Mare* is TB-25J USAAF s/n 44-86797 N3438G. The bomber was surplused in the early 1960s and went through a couple of owners but did little flying, spending much of its time on the ground at Tracy and Turlock, California, before being purchased by Aero Trader in 1973. Aero Trader kept the Mitchell in storage, gradually repairing corrosion and other damage before selling it to Sanders in 1984

Above Distinctive nose art and Japanese victory markings on *Ol Gray Mare*

Right Virtually obscured by Alaskan forest, the bleak remains of this Mitchell can only be spotted from the air. The aircraft, a TB-25N registered N9088Z, and owned by Ed Thorrude of Missoula, Montana, was on lease to the Bureau of Land Management in 1969 and operating as Tanker 8Z from Fairbanks International Airport. On 27 June 1969, while being flown by Herm Gallaher, the Mitchell experienced a power loss shortly after take-off. Gallaher found a fairly barren sand bar in the Tanana River and crash landed the tanker, tearing off the right wing in the process. The wreck was picked of its engines and a few other parts and then left where it slid to a stop. The river is constantly changing and over the years the sand bar became an island with a heavy growth of trees. In 1992, the author, along with Privateer fire bomber captain John Gallaher (Herm's son) flew in a BLM helicopter and located the nearly covered wreck which, by this time, had been hacked to pieces by locals, and landed for an examination of what was left. John was able to secure a few souvenirs in memory of his father, who passed away in 1986

Above N3155G was parked for many years at both Chino and nearby Ramona Airport following its withdrawal from fire bomber duties. Built as TB-25N USAAF s/n 44-30823, the Mitchell was restored to flying condition by Carl Scholl and Tony Ritzman of Aero Trader as the first Mitchell twin refurbished by the company, which would later become the world's main source of B-25 parts and airframes. The bomber was acquired by Don Davis of Casper, Wyoming, in 1980 and further work on the twin was carried out by Mike and Dick Wright (collectively known in warbird circles as the 'Wright Brothers'), and the B-25 emerged in an olive drab paint scheme with the name *Bronco Bustin' Bomber*. It is seen in flight during May 1984

Right TB-25N USAAF s/n 43-36074 N9079Z high over Geneseo on 16 August 1991 in company with a P-51D. The Mitchell, flown by Skip Leman and Rick Korff, is owned by the latter individual, as is the Mustang, which is being flown by Bill Dodds. This particular aircraft started out its civil life as a fire bomber (Tanker 32) and eventually wound up in the now defunct SST Aviation Museum (along with N2825B), before going to Tom Reilly for rebuild in the early 1980s. The B-25 emerged from the Kissimmee facility in March 1986, its aluminum skin highly polished and the attractive art of *Panchito* painted on the nose. On 18 August 1988, *Panchito* was landing at Wichita Falls, Texas, following a violent storm. The aircraft hydroplaned on the runway and went off one side, heavily damaging the vintage bomber. Fortunately, damage was repairable and with the help of a new nose, supplied by Aero Trader, N9079Z flew once again. Korff purchased the aircraft in 1991

Above One of the most accurate Mitchell restorations during the 1980s was TB-25N USAAF s/n 44-29887 N10564, owned and operated by Warbirds of the World in Dunnellon, Florida. Seen airborne during March 1985, the aircraft was finished in an accurate military scheme and fitted with the majority of its original equipment. In 1985, the Mitchell was donated to the National Air and Space Museum at Dulles Airport (where it is now stored in a hangar awaiting the possible construction of a new museum wing at Dulles), and its final flight was a wild one, with the owner/pilot having his pilot's ticket pulled by the FAA after flying *inside* a large football stadium while a game was in progress! This aircraft had operated with the Forest Service for many years as Tanker 91, and was restored to flying condition for *Catch 22*

Right One of the very first Mitchells to become a Warbird was TB-25N USAAF s/n 44-30801 N30801 (ex-N3699G). After being surplused, the aircraft went to Avery Aviation in Greybull, Wyoming, where work was undertaken to turn it into a crop sprayer and fire bomber. In 1968, the now derelict Mitchell was purchased by Tallmantz for the epic *Catch 22*, and flown to Orange County for further work before filming. After completion of the motion picture, '801 was sold to Ed Schnepf, who had the airframe restored back to its former military glory. The aircraft became an immediate hit on the airshow circuit, helping to kick off the warbird movement. Currently, Executive Sweet operates from Camarillo, California, in a different set of markings. The Mitchell is escorted by Schnepf's North American BT-9 (later donated to the USAF Museum) and *Tora! Tora! Tora!* Zero

Above Mike Pupich shakes hands with pilot Steve Crowe prior to launch. Four B-25s arrived at NAS North Island several weeks before the planned event and these included *Pacific Princess*, *Executive Sweet*, *In The Mood* and *Heavenly Body*. The bombers and crews were warmly greeted by the Navy, and intensive planning for the carrier launch took place. Crews were also trained in carrier techniques, and a portion of the North Island runway was marked off for take-off trails. The Mitchells had to launch in less than the available 900 ft on the *Ranger*'s deck (on the *Hornet*, Doolittle and his crews had only 450 ft of available deck), and the practice launches ranged from 700 ft to 580 ft, with the average being 600 ft. The two aircraft that would go aboard the *Ranger* would each carry 300 gallons of avgas. The aircraft chosen were *Heavenly Body* and *In The Mood*. *Executive Sweet* would serve as a standby in case of mechanical problems

Right On 21 April 1992, a most amazing event took place. Two Mitchells had been craned aboard the USS *Ranger* (CV-61) as the huge carrier docked at North Island in San Diego, California. While the placing of two vintage bombers aboard a carrier may be odd in itself, the mission was even stranger – to launch the two bombers from the carrier to commemorate the 50th anniversary of the Doolittle Raid against Japan. The two B-25s were carefully craned aboard the carrier several days previously and crews worked on the bombers to ensure that the aircraft were in perfect condition. The early morning light reflects off the olive drab paint of *Heavenly Body* as the *Ranger* waits to get underway. In a unique blend of civilian and military co-operation, the plans for the re-enactment of the Doolittle Raid were actually begun in 1989. The joint efforts of Bradley Grose, Joe Davis, and members of the Eagle Field Museum in Dos Palos, California, eventually resulted in the aircraft going aboard the carrier. The complex negotiations for such an ambitious project went ahead smoothly due to the US Navy's enthusiastic co-operation, and they helped turn the idea into reality

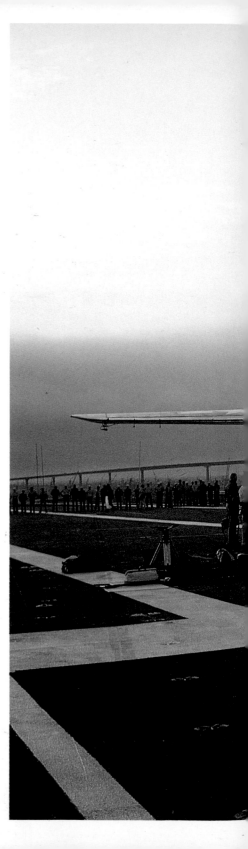

Above *Heavenly Body*'s gear comes up into the wells on a test flight prior to the carrier mission. TB-25N USAAF s/n 44-30748 N8195H originally operated with Avery Aviation as a sprayer and fire bomber, before becoming a film star in *Catch 22*. When the aircraft were put up for sale following completion of film work, '748 was purchased by Mike Pupich. As the morning of 21 April progressed, Capt Dennis V McGinn carefully took CV-61 out of port and headed for the open sea. Only a slight rolling motion was felt as the 80,000 ton carrier turned into the wind off the coast of San Diego. Well below deck,

the *Ranger*'s eight boilers were churning out more than 280,000 horsepower as the ship sliced through the ocean at 32 knots. Visitors aboard the carrier were startled by the sound of two cannon reports, signifying the sighting and sinking of a Japanese picket ship on the actual raid. From that point, the 'raid' was on. In *Heavenly Body*, Steve Crowe and Sam Pennington cranked over the R-2600s, which burst smoothly into life. *Aboard In The Mood*, William Klaers, Alan Wojciak, and Robert Lumbard did the same thing. Each engine was carefully monitored and run up to make sure all was well

Above After engine run-ups were completed, catapult officer Lt Greg Sullivan dropped to one knee and indicated to Crowe that it was time to launch. With engines at 44 inches of manifold pressure and full flaps, *Heavenly Body* surged forward to the cheers of the spectators. It was evident that within 100 ft the Mitchell was already riding lightly on its nose wheel, and the bomber smoothly lifted off within 600 ft. *In The Mood* followed a few minutes later without any problem. It was all over in a few seconds, but history had been made once again as Mitchells were launched from a carrier. Aboard *Ranger* for this historic event were several original Tokyo Raiders, including Doolittle's navigator, Mac MacClure, and Travis Hoover, pilot of the second B-25 to launch on the raid. Also along for the trip was Bill Gibson, the combat photographer who took the historic photos of the raid's launch. He was tasked with recreating his assignment on board the *Ranger*

Above Once the two Mitchells were airborne, they were joined by *Pacific Princess*, *Tootsie*, *Executive Sweet* and Vern Raburn's RAF Mitchell for repeated passes over the carrier as it returned to port

Left In between paint schemes, *Pacific Princess* roars up the California coast heading for Monterey, the location of Gen Doolittle's home. The bombers dropped thousands of flowers on the home of a true American hero

North American NA-62 Mitchell

B-25 to TB-25N, PBJ series and F-10

Type: medium bomber and attack with crew from four to six

Engines: (B-25A, B) two 1700 hp Wright R-2600-9 Double Cyclone 14-cylinder two-row radials: (C, D, G) two 1700 hp R-2600-13: (H, J, F-10), two 1850 hp (emergency rating) R-2600-29

Dimensions: span 67 ft 7 in (20.6 m): length (B-25A) 54 ft 1 in: (B, C, J) 52 ft 11 in (16.1 m): (G, H) 51 ft (15.54 m): height (typical) 15 ft 9 in (4.80 m)

Weights: empty (J typical) 21,100 lbs (9580 kg): maximum loaded (A) 27,100 lbs: (B) 28,640 lbs: (C) 34,000 lbs (15,422 kg): (G) 35,000 lbs (15,876 kg): (H) 36,047 lbs (16.350 kg): (J) normal 35,000 lbs, overload 41,800 lbs (18,960 kg)

Performance: maximum speed (A) 315 mph: (B) 300 mph: (C, G) 284 mph (459 km/h): (H, J) 275 mph (443 km/h); initial climb (A, typical) 1500 ft (460 m)/min; (late models, typical) 1100 ft (338 m)/min; service ceiling (A) 27,000 ft (8230 m); (late models, typical) 24,000 ft (7315 m); range (all, typical) 1500 miles (2414 km)

Armament: see text.

History: first flight (NA-40 prototype) January 1939; (NA-62, the first production B-25) 19 August 1940; (B-25G) August 1942

Bill Klaers flying *In The Mood* on the way to Doolittle's house. B-25J USAAF s/n 44-29199 N9117Z started out civilian life as a sprayer and tanker before becoming derelict at Mesa, Arizona. Bill Lumbard purchased the bomber in 1978 and began the long task of restoring the aircraft back to its present condition

Wooden Warrior

Arguably the most attractive twin-engined aircraft built by the Allies during World War 2, the de Havilland Mosquito was developed and built under great secrecy in order to create an aircraft superior to the machines being operated or developed by the *Luftwaffe*. The company had gained tremendous experience in building lightweight highly efficient civilian aircraft over the span of two decades, and many of these machines used wood to form a considerable part of their structure. Before the war, de Havilland built an elegant and very streamlined four-engined airliner named the Albatross. Although this aircraft was not a commercial success, the Albatross did give the company tremendous experience in construction techniques as it was built almost entirely out of wood, and offered exceptionally high performance.

At first, a smaller Albatross capable of carrying a bomb load to Berlin on two Rolls-Royce Merlin engines was considered, but this was stillborn until 1939 when the idea of a high performance twin-engined wooden bomber was proposed in detail. At first the concept was met by official reluctance as being too radical or unworkable, but on 1 March 1940, a contract was finally placed for 50 D.H.98 Mosquitos. Development was carried out at Salisbury Hall, an ancient structure outside of London, where

Left Canada contributed to the Mosquito war effort by opening a production line at de Havilland's Toronto factory and, as can be seen, Mosquitos were soon heading toward the war front. Note the fuselage hanging from the rafters *(de Havilland Aircraft of Canada/Joe Holliday)*

Right Few American civil registered Mosquitos survived long enough to enjoy continued survival via the warbird movement of the mid-1970s. Photographed during October 1963 at Whiteman Air Park in Los Angeles, FB Mk VI PZ474 arrived in LA during 1955 from New Zealand, where it had served as NZ2384 before being surplused in 1952 as ZK-BCV. Given the registration N9909F, the Mosquito began a quick slide downhill at Whiteman which was, at that time, a Mecca for odd and wonderful aircraft. The owner apparently had the misguided notion that he would strip all the fabric off the airframe and then recover it. However, once the fabric came off, he apparently lost interest and the Mosquito's wood was directly exposed to the weather. The aircraft eventually broke in two behind the wing trailing edge, and the remains were gradually vandalized until very little was left. The earthly bits and pieces of N9909F were purchased by Jim Merizan, who has collected an impressive array of other Mosquito wrecks and parts. By using composite technology and original parts, Merizan eventually hopes to create a flying Mosquito around the registration of N9909F. The Mitchells and Invader surrounding the 'Wooden Wonder' were scrapped during the late 1960s and early 1970s

design and construction could be done away from prying eyes.

The new aircraft was a very attractive design constructed of laminations of cedar ply sandwiching a layer of plywood. Streamlined nacelles housed two Rolls-Royce Merlin 21 engines of 1250 horsepower each. The new aircraft went together quickly, and painted yellow overall and carrying the serial W4050, made its first flight on 25 November 1940 with Geoffrey de Havilland at the controls – an amazingly short period from design to first flight. From the start, de Havilland and the RAF knew they had a winner and the Mosquito would go on to become the Allies' fastest operational aircraft for a good portion of the war. It was developed in many different variants and configurations, and the design's wartime exploits have filled numerous volumes. Today, Salisbury Hall is the home of the Mosquito Museum, and prototype W4050, along with several other marks, is lovingly preserved and on display for the public to enjoy.

The Mosquito was originally designed to carry a bomb load to the heart of Germany, but de Havilland and the RAF also knew that the aircraft could be developed to perform as a night fighter, a recon platform and also fulfil a variety of other missions. The Mosquito became operational in May 1942 and the design went on to expand and improve with time and changing military situations. Since the weapons bay on the bomber variant was rather small, the initial bomb load was planned at only 1000 lbs, but it was found that trimming the stabilizing fins on the 500 lb bomb meant that four of the weapons could be carried instead of just four 250 lb 'cookies' – thus doubling the aircraft's war load. Growth variants led to 'swelling' the bomb bay to carry more and larger weapons, while underwing fuel tanks were added to increase range as overall airframe weight grew.

Mosquitos were also license-built in Canada in order to increase production and the type was operated by the USAAF under Reverse Lend-Lease. Canada would go on to build 1134 Mosquitos, the majority of which were delivered to Britain by the northern ferry route. Australia also built Mosquitos under license and the type enjoyed great success in the Far East, although the hot and humid weather played havoc with its wooden structure. In total, 7781 Mosquitos of all types were constructed by the various countries involved, and the D.H.98 became one of the war's exceptional aircraft, participating in some of the most historic raids on the enemy.

After the conclusion of hostilities, the Mosquito soldiered on with the RAF and other air forces for a number of years, but surplus examples also began to appear on the civil registers of Britain, the United States, Canada, and Australia. Most of these aircraft were ostensibly to be used as high altitude mapping and survey platforms, but a number of the British civil registered examples were smuggled to the newly emerging Israeli Air Force. At least two American registered examples competed, unsuccessfully, in the Cleveland Air Races. Spartan Air Services in Canada made regular and efficient use of their Mosquitos on survey flights but, as the years went on, the Mosquito fleet began to dwindle due to accidents, high maintenance costs, and the availability of newer aircraft.

The RAF disposed of its last Mosquitos in the early 1960s, the small fleet of aircraft operated by the meteorological flight at Exeter being purchased lock, stock and barrel for the use in the film *633 Squadron*. A few of the survivors would show up in later years in the very forgettable *Mosquito Squadron*. Such was the value of the aircraft, that several Mosquitos were intentionally destroyed for the cameras. However, from this small group came several of today's Mosquito survivors.

In the United States, Mosquitos were mainly used for survey and mapping work by companies such as the IREX Survey Co and Fotogrametric Engineers. Other aircraft were imported for more esoteric, and sometimes shadowy, reasons. Some sources have stated that one or two US civil machines were utilized for covert operations by the Central Intelligence Agency. One of the most interesting of the American civil registered aircraft was Mosquito N1203V belonging to Dianna Bixby. This aircraft attempted an around-the-world record flight in 1950 but was beset with mechanical problems. Returned to its Burbank, California, base, the Mosquito, under the sponsorship of Flying Tiger Line, had its forward fuselage chopped off and a custom-designed section with pressurized cockpit fitted in its place. Bixby attempted another around-the-world flight in the highly modified aircraft during 1954 but this also failed. The final

Above Finished in accurate RAF camouflage and markings, Kermit Weeks brings B Mk 35 N35MK in close to the camera ship, illustrating such features as the tightly cowled Merlins, bulged bomb bay and bombardier's position. When Hurricane *Andrew* levelled the Weeks Air Museum in 1992, N35MK was on display at Oshkosh and escaped damage

fate of N1203V is not known and Ms Bixby died shortly after in the crash of her converted Douglas A-20 Havoc.

N9919F, a B Mk 35 ex-VR801, and N9909F, FB Mk VI ex-PZ474, were imported into the USA from New Zealand in the 1950s. Both aircraft were seldom, if ever, flown after their arrival and N9919F led a very chequered history and was part of an elaborate plot that involved a murder charge! The owner of the Mosquito had the aircraft (which was lapsing into dereliction at Burbank, California) heavily insured with Lloyds and arranged with a pilot to take-off from Burbank, fly over the Pacific, report over the radio that he had an inflight fire, and bail out. The owner would collect the insurance and give the pilot a cut, both making a decent profit from a few hours of work. However, when the Mosquito departed Burbank one of the Merlins actually did fail and, after apparently struggling to avoid built-up areas, crashed into the mountains near Calabasas, starting a

Above The bomber variant of the Mosquito was originally designed to be unarmed, relying on speed and surprise to escape *Luftwaffe* fighters – something it did with ease until the appearance of later variants of the Focke-Wulf Fw 190 and the German jets. The Mosquito was a growth aeroplane, the basic design evolving into a wide number of variants capable of performing every sort of aerial combat mission. As can be seen on Kermit's B Mk 35, the bulged bomb bay could accommodate a 4000 lb bomb, a far cry from the design's original 1000 lb bomb load. While this chapter was being written, Kermit Weeks was in Britain test flying his Short Sunderland flying boat, preparing the sole airworthy survivor for its flight across the Atlantic to · central Florida, where the combat veteran will join the massive new Weeks Air Museum that is currently being completed. The Mosquito is just one of many British aircraft obtained by the avid collector, and it is his dedication that results in American airshow audiences enjoying the unique sight and sound of a Mosquito in its natural element – the air

Left When RS712 was purchased from the Strathallan Collection, it had been painted in a postwar overall silver finish. When Personal Plane Services at Booker, England, overhauled the craft, a more war-like camouflage scheme was applied

fire and killing the pilot. An investigation quickly revealed the insurance scam and, after protracted legal work, the owner was finally tried and sent to jail.

As of the writing of this book, only two Mosquitos remain airworthy, although there is the chance that one or possibly two other airframes will once again fly provided sufficient financing and talent is made available to complete their restorations. Originally starting out life as a B Mk 35 and later being converted to TT Mk 35 status, Mosquito RS712 probably owes its survival to having been used in the making of *633 Squadron*. Registered G-ASKB, the aircraft survived the rigours of this particular film and went through several owners, fortunately being maintained in marginally flyable condition in the process, until being purchased by Sir Bunny Roberts for his Strathallan Collection in Scotland during 1972. A crew from the small museum got the Mosquito into flying shape and took the craft to

Since Kermit's B Mk 35 is in very good condition, the aircraft will remain flyable for some time to come. However, with just two flying examples of the type, enthusiasts should enjoy these classics while they can. There is the possibility that three more Mosquitos may eventually fly if funds permit their restoration

de Havilland Mosquito 1 to 43

Type: designed as a high-speed day bomber

Engines: (Mks II, III, IV and early VI) two 1230 hp Rolls-Royce Merlin 21 or (late FB VI) 1635 hp Merlin 25, (Mk IX) 1680 hp Merlin 72; (Mk XVI) Merlin 72 or 1710 hp Merlin 73 or 77; (Mk 30); 1710 hp Merlin 76, (Mk 33) 1640 hp Merlin 25; (Mk 34, 35, 36) 1690 hp Merlin 113/114. Many other variants had corresponding Merlins made by Packard

Dimensions: span (except Mk XV) 54 ft 2 in (16.5 m); length (most common) 40 ft 6 in (12.34 m); (bombers) 40 ft 9 ½ in; (radar-equipped fighters and Mks 34-38) typically 41 ft 9 in; (Mk 39) 43 ft 4 in; height (most common) 15 ft 3 ½ in (4.66 m)

Weights: empty (Mks II-VI) about 14,100 lbs; (Mks VIII-30) about 15,200 lbs; (beyond Mk 30) about 15,900-16,800 lbs; maximum gross (Mks II and III) around 17,500 lbs; (Mks IV and VI) about 22,500 lbs; (later night fighters) about 20,500 lbs but (HF XV) only 17,395 lbs; (Mks IX, XVI and marks beyond 30) typically 25,000 lbs (11,340 kg)

Performance: maximum speed, from 300 mph (TT 39 with M4 sleeve) to 370 mph (595 km/h) for early night fighters, 380 mph (612 km/h) for III, IV and VI, 410 mph (660 km/h) for IX, XVI and 30 and 425 mph for 34 and 35; service ceiling, from 30,000 ft (9144 m) for low-rated naval versions to 34,500 ft (10,520 m) for most marks, to around 40,000 ft (12,190 m) for high-blown versions, with Mk XV reaching 44,000 ft (13,410 m); combat range, typically 1860 miles (2990 km), with naval TFs down at 1260 miles and PR 34 up at 3500 miles

History: First flight 25 November 1940

its new home. However, the majority of the museum's assets were auctioned during 1981 and the Mosquito was purchased by American collector Kermit Weeks. He left the aircraft in Scotland for several years before ferrying it to Personal Plane Services, where Tony Bianchi and his engineers got the Mosquito back into fine flying shape. An epic ferry flight during October 1987 saw the Mosquito come to America as N35MK. Weeks has visited many airshows with the rare twin and it was fortunately on display at the Experimental Aircraft Museum in Oshkosh, Wisconsin, when Hurricane Andrew levelled the Weeks Air Museum at Tamiami, Florida, during 1992.

The only other airworthy Mosquito is T Mk III RR299 G-ASKH, which is owned and operated by British Aerospace. This vintage machine was the subject of a lengthy overhaul completed in 1992, and should be airworthy for many years to come. Given the nature of the D.H.98's construction, enthusiasts of warbirds should consider themselves lucky that the owners of these two fine aircraft keep them airworthy for spectators to enjoy.

Mighty Marauder

As with the Douglas A-20 dealt with earlier in this volume, the Martin B-26 Marauder was an aircraft that was built in large numbers and saw heavy military action with America and its Allies during World War 2, yet by the early 1950s the type was nearly extinct. During January 1939, the Army Air Corps issued a Request for Specific Proposal to aeronautical concerns interested in building a high-speed, twin-engined medium bomber. The specification demanded a high top speed, a bomb load of 2000 lbs, a crew of five and an armament of four .30 calibre Browning machine guns. Besides this rather bare bones concept, the rest was left to the manufacturers, who realized that a high top speed meant a high landing speed and, possibly, tricky handling characteristics. On 5 July 1939, the Glenn L Martin Co submitted a proposal to the Air Corps, along with the rather unusual guarantee to construct a number of aircraft in a given time period.

Designer Peyton Magruder had given Martin Model 179 the highest wing loading of any Army combat aircraft to date, but the military liked the design and ordered 201 examples under the designation B-26 Marauder. The aircraft had a graceful circular fuselage, two tightly cowled R-2800 radials and a rather small wing. The plexiglass nose contained a .30 calibre

Left Martin B-26 USAAC s/n 40-1464 N4297J runs up its R-2800 radials prior to an attempted first flight on 2 May 1991. Mechanical problems prevented the flight from taking place, much to the disappointment of many former Marauder crewmen who had gathered at Chino to witness the event. However, the fact that the aircraft was even on the ramp and running was an epic event in itself

Right The restoration of B-26 40-1464 was a drawn-out event with many starts and stops. By 5 August 1973, the Marauder had been partially assembled and was parked in Tallichet's compound at Chino. As can be seen, many components were missing. The Canadian weather had preserved the original Air Corps markings in almost perfect condition, but the corrosive Chino weather immediately began to take its toll on the original Olive Drab and Neutral Grey camouflage

weapon on a swivel mount, while a similar weapon was fitted in the tail. A Martin electrically operated top turret contained two .50 calibre machine guns. The wing was mounted atop the fuselage to leave the centre section free for bomb stowage and ease of crew movement.

The fact that there was no prototype Marauder was unusual, but the first aircraft off the production line in Baltimore, Maryland, were reserved for testing. The first B-26, USAAC s/n 39-1361, first flew on 25 November 1940 and in-depth testing began immediately. With a top speed of 315 mph and the ability to carry up to 5800 lb of bombs, the B-26A would be the fastest of all Marauder variants.

High top speed and high wing loading simply equated to a high landing speed and it was hoped that the aircraft's tricycle landing gear would help new pilots acclimate more easily to the aircraft. However, as the design progressed so did the weight, and conversion training to the type began taking much longer than planned and also started becoming more dangerous as accidents increased. The weight of the B-26A grew over one ton as more military equipment and extra armour was added.

During February 1942, Marauders of the 22nd Bombardment Group (Medium) deployed from Virginia to Australia to bolster Allied forces, since the threat of a Japanese invasion was very real. Marauders hit the Japanese for the first time at New Guinea in long-distance raids that limited the aircraft's bomb load. Still, the fact that the enemy could be bombed at will came a surprise to the Japanese. From that time, Marauders began to spread out over the battle map as more aircraft flowed from the

Baltimore factory. Training accidents began to give the type a bad reputation and an engine lost on take-off could spell disaster for a crew that did not react quickly.

Combat reports began to make changes on the production line and the B-26B featured increased armour protection, twin .50 calibres in the tail, revised cowlings and improved radios and avionics. Weight increased to 36,500 lbs, but more powerful R-2800-41/43 radials of 1920 hp were added as soon as they became available from Pratt & Whitney. From the B-26B-10 production block on, the wing span was increased from 65 to 71 ft in order to improve handling characteristics and make training easier and safer. However, as total wing area went up so did the overall weight, thus resulting in the actual advantage of this modification being of minimal value. Improvements were added continuously and the aircraft evolved into a formidable enemy – Saburo Sakai, one of Japan's top aces, lost an eye while engaging a Marauder in combat over the Pacific.

The aircraft received its baptism in combat over the Pacific, but by late 1942 Marauders were arriving in North Africa in large number to serve with the Ninth Air Force and participate in fierce air battles over North

Above By March 1977, the Marauder was basically still in a semi-complete configuration, the MARC crew spending much of its time working other projects held by the company

Right The three Marauders recovered from Canada were in remarkably complete condition and most of the original tags and placards were still in place

Africa, Italy, Sicily, Corsica, Sardinia and France. In action, the Marauder began to assemble an impressive combat record, which helped to dispel the reputation the type accrued in training.

By early 1943, Marauders began to arrive in Britain for the Eighth Air Force and the first B-26 strike from Britain took place on 14 May 1943 when a dozen 322nd Bomb Group Marauders hit Ijmuiden. Disaster was to strike just a few days later on 17 May when 11 B-26s attacked the same target and all were lost – a stunning blow to the Eighth. The entire Marauder force, as well as other light and medium bombers, was eventually transferred to the Ninth Air Force and began to gain success after success in the tactical support role.

Martin opened another plant in Omaha, Nebraska, where B-26Bs were built as B-26Cs. The B-26B/C was the most produced variant of the type, but improvements continued and the B-26G had its wing incidence increased in a hope to improve take-off performance, while further interior improvements were also added. Britain received Marauders under Lend-Lease while further examples went to the Free French forces. The final B-26G rolled off the Martin line on 18 April 1945 and by this time the aircraft's armament had increased to 11 .50 calibre guns and 4000 lbs of bombs.

With the conclusion of hostilities, the Air Force had little need for the B-26 Marauder since the type had been eclipsed by the newer and more efficient Douglas A-26. Rather than flying hundreds of aircraft back to the States from foreign bases, Marauders were simply blown apart with grenades and scrapped at their overseas bases. Those aircraft still in the United States were sent to storage yards for disposal by War Assets. Most Marauders were sold in lots for metal scrap.

However, a few Marauders did make it into civil hands and three were converted to B-26C-T executive transport configuration for the Tennessee Gas Transmission Co of Houston, Texas, by AirResearch of Los Angeles. The B-26Cs received executive interiors and large windows while the cowlings were rebuilt into more streamlined units and large nose and tail fairings were installed to improve streamlining. An airstair door was added for boarding convenience while numerous other airframe modifications helped increase the aircraft's top speed. The B-26C-Ts made good high-speed transports for hauling company executives across the US, but after one Marauder crashed on a flight, killing a number of company officers, the survivors were sold. Before conversion to B-26C-T status, USAAF s/n 41-35071 N5546N was flown in the 1949 Bendix as Race 24 *Valley Turtle*. After numerous owners and a variety of experiences and accidents, the aircraft is now owned by the CAF, whose volunteers have rebuilt to military specs, and the bomber now flies in USAAF markings as Carolyn.

David Tallichet owns one of the largest fleets of aircraft in the world and his main base is at Chino. During World War 2, Tallichet flew combat missions as a co-pilot in Flying Fortresses from Thorpe Abbotts and has, naturally, a warm affection for aircraft of that era. In the early 1970s, Tallichet was informed that three B-26s which had crash-landed in British Columbia on 15 January 1942 were still where they came down. A visit to the site proved that the aircraft were in remarkable condition – even the camouflage paint and national insignias appeared to be almost new. After the forced landing, the Army had removed much equipment but the airframes were essentially intact on the three aircraft (s/ns 40-1451, 40-1459, and 40-1464) and Tallichet decided to initiate a major expedition to recover the aircraft from the wilds of British Columbia during 1971.

The disassembly and recovery of the aircraft was accomplished under extreme hardship and the airframes were moved by hand, truck, helicopter and finally rail until they finally arrived at Ontario International Airport, just north of Chino. Upon arrival at Chino, one aircraft, 40-1464, was partially assembled and put on display, but work on the airframe was sporadic at best. The other airframes were put into storage and augmented by the discovery of two B-26B fuselages in nearby Pacific Palisades, where they had been in a backyard since 1949! A further Marauder nose section was discovered in a Hollywood movie studio where it had apparently been used in the wartime film *A Guy Named Joe*. This unit was also purchased and moved to Chino for storage in the Tallichet Military Aircraft Restoration Corp (MARC) yard.

Work on 40-1464 commenced in earnest during 1989 and the completed

Above David Tallichet, a former Flying Fortress co-pilot with the 100th Bomb Group in Britain during World War 2, is interviewed by the press on the occasion of the Marauder's roll-out. N4297J is one of just two airworthy B-26s, and the only short-wing variant

Above right With a complex vintage warbird like the Marauder, maintenance is an on-going mission – here, a mechanic is seen digging into the nose case of a Pratt & Whitney R-2800 radial. As of this writing, the Tallichet Marauder was undergoing regular flight testing from Chino, working off the normal 25 hour flight restriction imposed by the Federal Aviation Administration

Below right Highlighted by the bright pre-war national insignia, the electrically-operated Martin turret contains two replica .50 calibre machine guns

aircraft, registered N4297J, was rolled out for the press on 2 May 1991 for its first flight, but an engine malfunction prevented the event from taking place and the aircraft went back into the hangar for more work – it failed to make its first post-restoration flight until 18 April 1992. The B-26 is in amazingly stock condition and is the only flying example of a short wing Marauder. As of this writing, the aircraft has made around ten flights under the command of Ross Diehl and Tallichet, and they hope to have the machine fully operational for airshow flying by the end of 1993.

Marauder 40-1451 has been leased to Air Heritage Inc in Beaver Falls, Pennsylvania, along with several other Tallichet aircraft, where it is slowly being restored back to flying condition. Two B-26G Marauders still survive and these are 43-34581 in the USAF Museum and 44-68219 in storage for the *Musee de l'Air*. Both of these machines were obtained by Air France from the *Armee de l'Air* in 1951 and used to train apprentices until 1965, when they went to their respective museums.

Below This Marauder nose section was being offered for sale by Aero Trader at Chino during July 1993. The section, still carrying its original camouflage and what appears to be the remains of training unit codes, was believed to have been used in the war-time Spenser Tracy film *A Guy Named Joe*, which used Marauders as Japanese *Betty* bombers. The film was remade as *Always* in 1989

The National Air and Space Museum in Washington DC has the nose of B-26B 41-31773 on display. This aircraft is the famous combat veteran *Flak Bait* and the remainder of the airframe is stored at the museum's Silver Hill facility awaiting restoration. Thus, as can be seen, the Marauder is a very rare survivor with just two flying examples that may, eventually, be joined by a third.

Above Howard Smiley was the co-pilot of Marauder 40-1464 when it went down on 16 January 1942 in British Columbia, and he was injured in the crash. Smiley and his pilot elected to land gear down, which was a mistake as the nose gear was torn out, the nose mangled and both men injured. However, the remainder of the airframe was in good shape and, with the help of a nose from one of the other B-26s, Tallichet made the decision to get 40-1464 back into the air. Smiley is seen with 'his' aircraft on 2 May 1991

Martin B-26 Marauder

Model: 179, B-26A to G, Marauder 1 to 111
Type: five- to seven-seat medium bomber
Engines: two Pratt & Whitney Double Wasp 18-cylinder two-row radials; (B-26) 1850 hp R-2800-5; (A) 2000 hp R-2800-39; (B, C, D, E, F, G) 2000 hp R-2800-43
Dimensions: span (B-26, A and first 641 B-26Bs) 65 ft (19 8 m); (remainder) 71 ft (21 64 m); length (B-26) 56 ft. (A, B) 58 ft 3 in (17-75 m); (F, G) 56 ft 6 in (17 23 m); height (up to E) 19 ft 10 in (6 04 m); (remainder) 21 ft 6 in (6 55 m)
Weights: empty (early, typical) 23,000 lbs (10,433 kg); (F, G) 25,300 lbs (11,490 kg); maximum loaded (B-26) 32,000 lbs; (A) 33,022 lbs; (first 641 B) 34,000 lbs, then 37,000 lbs (16,783 kg); (F) 38,000 lbs; (G) 38,200 lbs (17,340 kg)
Performance: maximum speed (up to E, typical) 310 mph (500 km/h); (F, G) 280 mph (451 km/h); initial climb 1000 ft (305 m)/min; service ceiling (up to E) 23,000 ft (7000 m); (F, G) 19,800 ft (6040 m); range with 3000 lbs (1361 kg) bomb load (typical) 1150 miles (1850 km)
Armament: (B-26, A) five 0.30 in or 0.50 in Browning in nose (1 or 2), power dorsal turret (2), tail (1, manual) and optional manual ventral hatch; (B to E) one 0.5 in manually aimed in nose, twin-gun turret, two manually aimed 0.5 in waist guns, one 'tunnel gun' (usually 0.5 in), two 0.5 in fitted in power tail turret, and four 0.5 in fixed as 'package guns' on sides of forward fuselage; (F, G) same but without tunnel gun; some variations and trainer and Navy versions unarmed. Internal bomb load of 5200 lbs (2359 kg) up to 641 st B, after which rear bay was disused (eliminated in F, G) to give maximum load of 4000 lbs (1814 kg). Early versions could carry two torpedoes
History: first flight 25 November 1940; service delivery 25 February 1941; final delivery March 1945

Above The only other flying Marauder has also been a hard luck aircraft, but it is also a survivor. Surplused as N5546N, the machine participated in the 1949 Bendix cross-country speed dash and was eventually turned into a highly modified executive transport, with the designation B-26C-T. Sold in Mexico as XB-LOX, the aircraft was returned to the States and damaged in a landing accident. Acquired by the CAF, it was moved to Harlingen and very heavily damaged in a take-off accident when the landing gear retracted. As can be seen, the wing is bent and other damage is also evident. The bomber was in poor condition and eventually moved into a hangar, where thousands of hours of work went into restoring it back into a more military configuration. The B-26 flew once again on 11 September 1984, but suffered a nose gear collapse on 12 October 1985 and required further repairs. As of this writing, the Marauder is airworthy and flying regularly, a considerable improvement on this October 1975 view

Elegant Invader

The Douglas A-26 Invader served America well through three major air wars and today remains one of the most numerous of surviving Bombing Twins. In many respects, the Douglas A-20 Havoc was a limited aircraft and a reflection of its mid-1930s design ethic. The company wanted to create a much faster, more heavily armed machine, and designer Ed Heinemann got to work on what would become the Invader. Due to the pressure of the international situation, the new design was ordered off the drawing board on 2 June 1941 and, as work began on prototype aircraft, a massive order for 500 production machines followed on 31 October of the same year.

The A-26 made its maiden flight on 10 July 1942, and it shared its twin engine, tricycle landing gear configuration with the A-20, but that was about all. The large, but sleek, warrior had a high aspect ratio wing with a laminar flow airfoil (like the P-51 Mustang), double slotted flaps, and two big Pratt & Whitney R-2800s in tight cowls. With the war now encompassing the globe, work on the A-26 proceeded at a maximum pace, with the second prototype being fitted out as a night fighter and the third boasting a 75 mm T-7 cannon. The R-2800s had large spinners on the prototypes, but these were deleted on the production aircraft.

Left Invaders pour off the Douglas production line at the company's Long Beach factory

Right Although not as common a twin as the B-25 Mitchell, the A-26 is increasing in number in warbird circles as more of the powerful attack bombers are restored by discerning owners. Conair of British Columbia operated a large fleet of Invader fire bombers up until 1986 when the fleet was retired or sold off to the USAF Museum. A-26C USAAF s/n 44-35752 was sold surplus in the early 1960s to the Rock Island Oil & Refining Co of Wichita, Kansas, who, at one time, owned numerous Invaders. This particular aircraft received the civil registration N8627E and stayed in fairly stock condition until sold to Conair in 1973, where it was suitably modified for fire bombing and given the Canadian registration CF-KBZ and operated as Tanker 28. The bomber was later transferred to the Canadian Warplane Heritage in Mount Hope, Ontario, but put up for sale. It was sold to Vern Raburn, who stripped out the fire bombing equipment, although when this August 1989 photograph was taken, standard bomb bay doors had not yet been fitted. The B-26's aluminum skin was highly polished and replica gun barrels were added to the nose. As can be seen in this chapter, the gun noses came in different configurations from the factory, and this particular fitment has the weapons spread out horizontally. Now registered N81797, the Invader is seen over the attractive countryside near Geneseo

The first Invaders came from the Long Beach factory in the standard USAAF Olive Drab and Neutral Grey camouflage, but this was quickly dropped and the bare aluminum skin gave the streamlined Invader an even more powerful appearance. The first production aircraft, appearing in September 1943, were fitted with the cannon, but this was quickly changed to an all-purpose nose section that housed eight .50 calibre machine guns (A-26B) or an easily interchangeable glass bombardier's unit (A-26C). Many minor improvements were made on the production line as tempo built but the basic design would remain unchanged throughout its production life.

The Invader had a very large bomb bay that could hold six 500 lb bombs or four 1000 lb bombs. In order to accommodate more production, a new Invader factory was built at Tulsa, Oklahoma, and it began delivering aircraft in January 1944. Right from the beginning, the Invader was a very heavily armed attack bomber. Four underwing packs each containing two .50 calibre weapons could be fitted to earlier variants, while later aircraft had six .50 calibre guns built into the wing. Two power turrets held a total of four guns, while the eight .50 calibre nose installation meant that Invaders could carry up to 20 Browning air-cooled machine guns! The aircraft's high speed and very good manoeuvrability meant that it was a tough target for enemy fighters, and Invader crews often met and defeated Bf 109s and Fw 190s over their own territory. The Invader's worst enemy, as it was with all medium bombers, was flak.

Left Certainly the most authentic of all Invader restorations, A-26B USAAF s/n 41-30401 N39401 (ex-N3457G) is seen in flight during August 1985. This particular aircraft arrived at Van Nuys, California, in the late 1950s, and sat unconverted for many years. Gradual restoration work started on the bomber in the 1970s for a projected film, but did not get all that far. Activity increased on the rebuild front following its purchase by Challenge Publications in 1982, and the first post-restoration flight took place from Van Nuys on 18 August 1983 under the supervision of crew chief Nelson Knuedeler. Since the aircraft had never been demilitarized, most of the original service equipment fitted by Douglas was still intact, including the huge electric motor that powered the two gun turrets. Also, all the original armament wiring and fittings were still in place, so Whistler's Mother, as the Invader had been named, was basically ready to go to war once again. During World War 2, '401 flew with the 643rd Bomb Squadron, 409th Bomb Group, for 30 combat missions. The Invader, redesignated B-26 in 1947, went to war again in Korean and flew a further 100 combat missions before returning back home to serve with the 180th Tactical Reconnaissance Squadron of the Missouri ANG

On 29 March 1944, a stunning order for 5000 additional Invaders was received by Douglas and this included provisions for advanced and redesigned variants. The Invader's initial combat experiences were with the Ninth Air Force in Britain, the first mission being flown on 17 November 1944. As increasing numbers of A-26s flowed from the factories, more Invaders began to attack targets all over Occupied Europe. The complete collapse of Germany precluded the Invader from gaining even more combat honours, but the type saw considerable use in the Pacific, where its long range and reliable engines were much appreciated for over-water missions. The atomic bomb brought a premature end to the huge Invader contracts, but a respectable 2451 aircraft had nevertheless been delivered by the company.

The end of World War 2 did not spell the end of the Invader in military service. Since the aircraft was more advanced than other similar twins, all A-26s were eventually returned from overseas bases and not simply destroyed. A few did show up on the surplus market, but the Invader went on to serve with frontline, reserve and ANG units for years to come.

With North Korea's sudden invasion of South Korea the Invader was once again sent into combat. At this time, the USAF had 1054 A-26s but many were in storage and had to be prepared for flight and combat operations in what would become a hotly contested war once China entered the conflict. Invaders (by this time they had be redesignated as B-26s since the Marauder was long out of service) flew their first combat mission of the Korean War on 28 June 1950 when aircraft of the 3rd Bomb Wing attacked rail targets. The Invader was a 'jack of all trades' during the

Above The two power turrets on the Invader could move with incredible speed, making acquisition and firing at enemy fighters much easier. As can be seen in this rear angle, the four .50 calibre Brownings offered an excellent field of fire to cover the A-26's entire rear section. It took over 5000 man hours to get Whistler's Mother back into the condition seen in this photograph. The bomber is equipped with four underwing gun packs, each holding two .50 caliber machine guns. The twin power turrets were also equipped with two similar weapons each, and the gunner sat in the rear fuselage, where he controlled his turrets via a highly effective periscope system . In 1987, the aircraft was sold to the Weeks Air Museum where it was seldom flown and, unfortunately, in 1992 the Invader was heavily damaged by Hurricane *Andrew*

Above During World War 2, the airfield at Red Deer, Alberta, Canada, vibrated with the drone of RCAF Harvards training pilots for the air forces of the Commonwealth. Today, the airfield still has the appearance of a war-time base since it is home to Air Spray Ltd, who operate 17 Invaders out of the large wooden hangars that once housed the training aircraft. Air Spray uses its A-26s for fire bombing all over Canada, and during the off season the twins gather at Red Deer for maintenance and storage. This April 1990 view shows some of the fleet on the line prior to dispersal to remote fire bases. Tanker 4 C-FTFB is RB-26C USAAF s/n 44-3544, which started out life on the US civil register as N7656C, but has been operating with Air Spray since 1971. As can be seen, the glass nose has simply been painted over

Above Air Spray is always on the look out for Invader spares since it intends to keep its fleet operational for many years to come. This unusual creation is the one-off Lockheed Air Service (LAS) Super 26. This aircraft originally appeared on the civil register in 1954 as N5052N, and was rebuilt to the Super 26 standard at Ontario, California, in 1960. LAS, the airframe modification offshoot of the Burbank firm, was attempting to cash in on Invader conversions to executive transports. LAS disposed of the fuselage and created a new pressurized, deeper unit with a ring spar and Constellation canopy and cockpit components. A long nose was also added, along with upgraded CB radials,

but a market was not found for the craft and only one example was built. The aircraft eventually became N52NM and passed through several owners, before taking up Mexican registration XB-SIJ and the name *Koba Wiki*. By 1980, the aircraft had been grounded at San Antonio, its interior stripped in a search for drugs, and a large crack had appeared in one of its wing spars. In 1981, the airframe was purchased by Air Spray, who needed one of the wing panels for a damaged tanker. A crew went to Texas, placed a strap on the wing spar and then very gingerly flew the Super 26 back to Red Deer, where it was taken apart for spares. Its carcass was photographed in the Air Spray yard during April 1990

Above The rugged Invader airframe was put to many other trying duties beside the hazardous task of fire bombing. Because of its long range, good load carrying abilities and high speed, A-26s were used and modified for many missions. Over the years, Aero Service Corp of Philadelphia, Pennsylvania, used a variety of surplus military aircraft for specialized duties, and these aircraft included the Flying Fortress that is now owned and operated by the CAF. A-26C USAAF s/n 43-22612 N3710G was purchased by Aero Service in 1969 and extensively modified for global survey work, with a magnetometer in a tail boom along with other associated equipment in the fuselage. The nose had also been modified to include an auxiliary power unit, and the craft was seen at Van Nuys Airport on 30 March 1973 after the company had become a division of multi-national Litton

Industries. Aero Service moved its various aircraft and offices to Van Nuys in a short-lived attempt to become a West Coast company but the venture failed. The well-worn N3710G then passed through several of the more unsavoury characters that populate the warbird field and arrived in Britain during 1978 to be operated by the so-called Cavalier Air Force. By this time, the machine had acquired a pseudo-USAAF scheme, and some of the modifications such as the tail boom had been removed. On 21 August 1980, a pilot who had been doing low-level aerobatics, and who had been seeing a doctor for mental problems, flew the Invader straight into the ground at the Biggin Hill Airshow after entering an unrecoverable high speed stall, killing both himself and a number of passengers in a massive and well-publicized explosion

Left By the 1970s, the warbird movement had really 'taken off' and airframes were being saved around the world for preservation and restoration. However, this did not apply to the Invader. Tucson International Airport in Arizona had been a gathering place for surplus A-26s since Hamilton Aircraft, located at the field, performed work on the type for foreign air forces and civilian operators. This incredible tail-to-tail line up of Invaders was just a portion of the A-26 fleet stored at Tucson when photographed during June 1970 and, as can be clearly seen, represent a wide variety of markings. The aircraft were used for parts and to provide operational airframes when needed but when the demand began to dry up as the decade wore on, the twins were simply hacked apart for scrap and not even retained for spares

Right During the late 1960s and early 1970s many Invaders were simply abandoned around the country as maintenance either became too expensive or newer aircraft became available to fulfil their mission. This fate befell A-26C USAAF s/n 44-35710 N7705C, which had lapsed into dereliction before being ferried into Chino during the late 1970s. There, the aircraft continued to rot until some maintenance was performed on it prior to a proposed trade to the USAF Museum. During an attempted take-off, an R-2800 failed and the bomber has remained at Chino ever since in open storage. The aircraft appears to have had a partial On Mark conversion

Korean War, performing strafing, bombing and recon missions with equal dependability and professionalism. During the Korean War, Invaders flew 60,096 combat sorties, while RB-26s completed 11,944 recon missions. Invaders also performed the last combat and recon flights of the war.

After Korea, the Invader stayed in frontline service for a while longer, but many ANG units were equipped with the type. Surplus aircraft were provided to friendly countries such as France, where the aircraft was heavily used in action in Algeria and Indochina. In the early 1960s, a few Invaders were despatched to South Vietnam to join what would become a massive American build-up. The Invaders were used in clandestine missions by the 1st Air Commando Squadron, but by early 1964, the B-26s had been grounded because of age and structural failures.

Since numerous Invaders were still held in storage, and since the type was such an effective attack aircraft, the USAF issued a contract to On Mark Engineering at Van Nuys, California, to construct a highly modified Invader optimised for the Vietnam mission. On Mark had gained considerable Invader experience with its wide variety of executive A-26 conversions, and the B-26K Counter-Invader was completely rebuilt with a strengthened wing and fuselage, upgraded P&W R-2800-103W radials with reversible propellers, up to 14 fixed .50 calibre guns and eight substantial underwing pylons that could carry just about everything in the USAF inventory. The prototype first flew on 28 January 1963 and the USAF ordered 40 production examples from the small Van Nuys plant. The Invader, redesignated A-26A in 1967, proved useful in South-east Asia, especially for attacking enemy rolling stock at night on the infamous Ho Chi Minh Trail. When the type was withdrawn from service in 1969, survivors were flown back to Davis-Monthan AFB for storage and scrapping.

A few VB-26s soldiered on with the National Guard Bureau until the early 1970s when they were withdrawn, and the Invader's amazing military career with the USAF finally came to an end. The ultimate Invader book has yet to be written but the type saw combat in many third world areas

and some examples continued in military use until the early 1980s.

The Invader, in pre-Learjet days, became a desirable executive transport and numerous companies converted the type into a high-speed transport with On Mark being the most successful. The Invader was also widely used as a fire bomber, but it is today a collectable warbird. Stock examples are difficult to find and conversion back to original military status is difficult and expensive.

Above One of the few aircraft to survive the Tucson scrappings was this unidentified example (and escaped is only a relative term since the wings and tail have been torched off), which was photographed on 1 December 1992 in the Pima Air Museum storage compound, where it is held with a number of other aircraft in equally poor condition. The insignia on what's left of the vertical fin is 'The Devil's Own – Grim Reapers', which could make the bomber a Korean War veteran

Above On Mark Engineering won a contract to convert B-26s to the new Counter-Invader configuration for the expanding Vietnam conflict. The new aircraft was designated the B-26K and was a mean machine by any standard. Completely rebuilt with more powerful CB engines, strengthened wings, numerous underwing pylons and heavy armament, the B-26Ks (the designation was, confusingly, later changed to A-26A) undertook important missions in South-east Asia, but when the survivors were returned to Davis-Monthan AFB for storage, an order was given that the aircraft would not be released for public sale. The Counter-Invaders were methodically cut apart every few feet to insure that the were unusable (apparently, some of the bureaucrats feared that radicals would get a hold of the bombers and wage war with Cuba, etc), and precious few survived for preservation as a result

Right Arthur 'Wally' McDonnell managed to get a couple A-26A Counter-Invaders that the bureaucrats had transferred to the State of Georgia Forestry Commission for conversion to fire bombers. The aircraft were never converted and McDonnell bought two of the machines and ferried them back to his home base at Mojave, California. On arrival in Georgia, one of the aircraft had its nose gear collapse (a fault that plagued the entire Invader series) and was pulled onto the ramp and left. The other aircraft were also simply parked and never converted. Still in its original 603rd SOS, 1st SOW markings and camouflage, USAF s/n 64-17657 (formerly USAAF s/n 43-22649) carries the small civil registration N99218 under the horizontal tail. With smoke trailing from the R-2800s, the aircraft is seen taxying at Mojave on 23 March 1975 prior to a local flight

Above During February 1978, McDonnell survived an amazing crash in N99218 when, on short finals to Chino, one of the propellers went into reverse without any warning and the aircraft slammed into the ground, destroying itself in the process. Witnesses stated that McDonnell was out and running before most of the pieces had slid to a halt! Wally had a very lucky escape judging by what was left of a once-proud warrior. Reportedly, pieces of this machine were shipped to Britain to aid in another Invader restoration. Currently, only one Counter-Invader remains in civil hands – N4988N USAF s/n 64-17679 is owned and flown by Denny Lynch of Billings, Montana

Above A-26B USAAF s/n 41-39427 was one of the earliest civil registered Invaders, emerging as N75Y in 1954 and owned by the Texas Railroad Equipment Co. By 1969, the bomber had become N240P and had been modified into executive configuration. On 10 May 1977 it was acquired by the CAF, and eventually assigned to its Waco Wing. Lots of hard work has gone into the aircraft, and an eight-gun nose has been added along with all an-black USAF Korean War scheme

Right This extremely attractive Invader almost ended up in the scrap heap. The aircraft, discovered in Brazil minus engines and many other components, was purchased by Don Davis, who sent Mike and Dick Wright to South America with a couple of new R-2800s to get the twin back into flying condition. A-26B USAAF s/n 44-34749 was surplused in the early 1960s to Rock Island Oil & Refining, but went to Hamilton Aircraft in Tucson instead for convertion to approximate B-26K standards. In 1969 it was sent to the *Forca Aerea Brasileira* as B-26C 5174 (see Osprey's *Bombing Iron* volume for a photograph of this aircraft on pages 38-39). After being withdrawn from military use, 5174 was used as an instructional airframe before being pushed out into the weeds. It took the Wright brothers several months of hard work, but they eventually flew the bomber, now registered N4959K, back to home base at Casper, Wyoming, to complete the restoration. The aircraft is seen taking off at Breckenridge with the Wright brothers at the controls during May 1986. Currently owned by Abrams Airborne Manufacturing and operated from Avra Valley Airport north of Tucson, Arizona, N4959K is one of a small but growing number of Invaders flying in basically stock military condition

Left If you are going to fly an Invader, then you are going to need lots of knowledgeable maintenance people. After an aborted take-off at Breckenridge during May 1990, mechanics dig into 41-39427's offending Pratt & Whitney R-2800 radial to discover the problem. During the war, huge amounts of spares were built for military aircraft and engines, and enough of these spares still exist for the engines to keep running for many, many years to come. However, the main problem in flying vintage warbirds may come from the availability of avgas, as today's 100LL decreases the original power ratings. Future environmentally correct fuels may have an even worse effect on large aero engines

Above A-26B USAAF s/n 41-39161 N26RP is the oldest Invader still flying. First registered to Humphrey's Gold Corp during 1956 as N317V (later changing to N317W), the aircraft was later modified by On Mark into executive configuration. Purchased by Robert Lammerts of Oklahoma City during 1981, the aircraft was externally restored to military configuration as N26RP with an eight gun solid nose and two turret shells with replica .50 calibre weapons. As can be seen, the On Mark windows are still in place but a vintage ADF 'football' has been added atop the fuselage

Above During their moment of glory in the late 1950s and early 1960s, the On Mark Invaders were just about the fastest way to get around the country. The aircraft were usually beautifully maintained by the companies that owned them, and On Mark A-26B USAAF s/n 41-39516 N237Y is seen at Columbus, Ohio, during July 1970, still in fine condition. Originally owned by Standard Oil of Chicago, Illinois, the bomber was being operated by PBF Enterprises of Akron, Ohio, when photographed and shows the On Mark long nose, tip tanks, airstair door and vortex generators on the vertical tail. This aircraft was obtained by Calspan Corp of Buffalo, New York, and heavily modified into a control configured vehicle, where by the control forces of different aircraft could be programmed into the Invader's controls for use by test pilots at Edwards AFB. As of this writing, the aircraft was in poor condition and being offered for sale by the National Warplane Museum in Geneseo, New York

Above For many years, the Invader remained a very popular fire bomber in the United States, but the last examples were retired from active service by Lynch Air Tankers in Billings, Montana, during 1992. A-26B USAAF s/n 44-34508 N74874 is seen at the On Mark engineering facility at Van Nuys during January 1970 when it, along with several other A-26s, was receiving maintenance and spar modifications. At the time, Tanker 74 and the other Invaders at On Mark were owned by Rosenbalm Aviation of Medford, Oregon. Note that the fuel tanks have been pulled from the aircraft, which is otherwise basically in stock condition

Above RB-26C USAAF s/n 44-35323 N8026E operated as an air tanker with a number of companies during the 1960s and 1970s (including a spell as CF-CDD with Conair). Seen at Chino Airport during August 1980, the aircraft still wears full Aero Union Corp markings as Tanker 55. The twin was donated to The Air Museum in July 1980, and since that time the museum's volunteer force has restored N8026E back into military shape with a glass nose and Korean War markings

Above A-26B USAAF s/n 44-34609 N4819E is seen at Buckeye, Arizona, on 26 October 1990, heavily vandalized and with, according to locals, a cracked spar. Originally registered to the Rock Island Oil & Refining Co, N4819E was apparently going to be converted into a fire bomber, hence the crude drooped wing leading edge and wing fences. The bomber has been an attraction at the small Buckeye Airport for many years

Above During the 1950s and 60s, many firms got into the Invader executive conversion business, all with varying degrees of success. One of the most modified variants was the LB Smith Tempo II, which was a distinctive looking creation by any standards. Engineers at Smith basically threw away the A-26's fuselage and created a new stretched unit that was greatly increased in height and depth. It was also pressurized and a new cockpit and canopy installed. The wing was fitted with a ring spar to permit easier access through the cabin, tip tanks for extra range and CB engines and paddle blade props were added for increased performance. Only a few examples were built and sold, certainly not enough to cover the costs of engineering and tooling. Smith Tempo II A-26C USAAF s/n 44-35640 N4204A is seen when owned by the University of Nevada, Reno. The University purchased the aircraft in 1969 and carried out further heavy modifications, which are clearly for weather research. Seen during June 1979, the aircraft's Smith airstair door in the side of the fuselage allowed easy cabin access. During February 1980, while investigating weather build-ups, the Invader was torn apart by turbulence, killing the pilots and scientists aboard the craft

Left On Mark Marksman A-26B USAAF s/n 44-34766 N9150 has enjoyed a long and interesting career. Surplused in 1947, the Invader was initially registered as N67807 and participated in the 1948 and 49 Bendix cross-country speed dash. In the early 1950s, the aircraft was purchased by the Stanolind Oil & Gas Co, who in turn passed it to the Pan American Petroleum Corp as N1243 in 1954. By 1960, it had been modified by On Mark and was flown by the Nine Ten Corp as N910G. The aircraft had passed to the Paramount Trading Co by 1968 as N9150, and it is seen in that company's markings during May 1977 at Van Nuys Airport, with the name *Amazones* on the extended On Mark nose. By this time, the machine had gone through several different owners and was operating rather questionable flights 'down south'

Above By January 1978, N9150 sported a 'warbird' camouflage scheme, had had its wing tip tanks removed, and was operating on fairly regular drug flights from Van Nuys and other locations in company with a few other tired B-25s and A-26s. This chancy occupation was being performed directly under the eyes of the local Feds, who were either too stupid to notice, or were turning a blind eye for other reasons. By 1979, the bomber had been impounded and had become the property of the USAF Museum, who displayed it at Castle AFB

Left For some reason, N9150 came back on the civil market in 1984 and passed to the Donald Douglas Museum at Santa Monica. It had by now received an eight-gun nose, a general clean-up and a new paint scheme. Seen over California's central valley during August 1988, the craft passed to the new Museum of Flying at Santa Monica, but was sold in 1990

Left N9150 was purchased by warbird collector David Brady of Cartersville, Georgia, and named *Georgia Invader*. On 7 June 1991, while on the way to an airshow, Brady, flying in his civilianized Cessna T-37, misjudged a high speed pass at the A-26 and rammed the Invader, killing both himself and his passenger in the process. The Invader flew about for a while as the pilot checked out damage, which was fortunately minimal, and then made a safe landing. The bomber is seen at Van Nuys on 14 April 1993, after it had been purchased by Howard Keck

Above right The top of the line On Mark had a completely rebuilt fuselage that was pressurized as well as expanded to give 'stand up' head room. Equipped with R-2800-CB engines, reversible paddle-blade propellers, wing tip tanks, an extended nose and vertical tail and numerous other modifications, the machine was the ultimate On Mark model. Only a few were built and A-26B USAAF s/n 44-34526 N26AB is seen in open storage at Santa Teresa, New Mexico, on 30 May 1993 – this aircraft is possibly the last intact survivor of its breed. It has worn numerous civil identities over the years including N827W, N551EH, N400V and N7977. The weathered pseudo-military paint scheme includes nose art, as well as the DC-7 windshield that was grafted on to the pressurized On Marks

Douglas Invader

A-26 (later B-26) and JD-1 Invader; rebuilt as B-26K, redesignated A-26A
Type: three-seat attack bomber; FA-26 reconnaissance, JD target tug
Engines: two 2000 hp Pratt & Whitney R-2800-27, 71 or 79 Double Wasp 18-cylinder two-row radials; On Mark B-26K, 2500 hp R-2800-103W
Dimensions: span 70 ft (21.34 m) (B-26K, 75 ft, 22.86 m, over tip tanks); length 50 ft (15.24 m); height 18 ft 6 in (5.64 m)
Weights: empty, typically 22,370 lbs (10,145 kg): loaded, originally 27,000 lbs (12,247 kg) with 32,000 lbs (14,515 kg) maximum overload, later increased to 35,000 lbs (15,876 kg) with 38,500 lbs (17,460 kg) maximum overload
Performance: maximum speed 355 mph (571 km/h): initial climb 2000 ft (610 m)/min: service ceiling 22,100 ft (6736 m): range with maximum bomb load 1400 miles (2253 km)
Armament: (B-26B) ten 0.5 in Brownings, six fixed in nose and two each in dorsal and ventral turrets; internal bomb load of 4000 lbs (1814 kg), later supplemented by underwing load of up to 2000 lbs (907 kg); (B-26C) similar but only two 0.5 in in nose; (B-26K, A-26A) various nose configurations with up to eight 0.5 in or four 20 mm, plus six 0.30 in guns in wings and total ordnance load of 8000 lbs (3629 kg) in bomb bay and on eight outer-wing pylons
History: first flight (XA-26) 10 July 1942; service delivery December 1943; final delivery 2 January 1946; first flight of B-26K, February 1963

Vengeance From Vega

Hundreds of books have been written about the wartime exploits of aircraft such as the Mustang, Mitchell, Flying Fortress, Thunderbolt and Liberator, yet, distressingly few volumes document the aggressive combat history of two rough and tumble warriors that rolled off of Lockheed's Burbank production line – the PV-1 Ventura and the PV-2 Harpoon. Historic Burbank Airport is now basically that in just name only, for as this book was being completed in July 1993, bulldozers and wrecking cranes had been busy demolishing most of what once was Lockheed – including even the windowless building housing the famed 'Skunk Works', where so many aircraft important to the Free World were developed, including the P-38 Lightning, P-80 Shooting Star, U-2 Dragon Lady, SR-71 Blackbird and F-117A 'Nighthawk'. I can remember in the early 1960s when portions of the Lockheed factory still had their World War 2-vintage camouflage paint. Now, however, it is basically all gone as the 'Skunk Works' retrenches in Palmdale and major aircraft manufacturing moves to Georgia. The purchase of General Dynamics in 1993 means that Lockheed Fort Worth now has a huge fighter plant, but who knows how the dictates of a world economy will respond from countries no longer threatened by what was the Soviet Union.

It is difficult to drive down Hollywood Way, the main street bordering the east end of the field, and attempt to imagine what it must have been like during those dark early days of the 1940s as tens of thousands of workers swarmed into the expanding Lockheed plant to build what would become some of the most respected combat aircraft of that conflict. Photographic displays inside the terminal (which in itself houses the remains of the original 1930s' Spanish style terminal and is scheduled for destruction to make way for a new, safer terminal that is not so close to the runway) show what it looked like five decades ago in black and white

Left Fresh from the Burbank factory, a camouflaged PV-2 Harpoon is seen on a test flight prior to delivery to the US Navy. Since the Walt Disney film headquarters was also in Burbank, it was not uncommon for Venturas and Harpoons to have comic/patriotic art work added by Disney artists while the machines were on the production line. Oddly, the majority of this work was painted on the fuselage rather than on the nose, and an example can be seen behind the national insignia on this aircraft *(Lockheed)*

images, but trying to apply the imagination to acres of bulldozed ground and disappeared landmarks is difficult at best.

The PV-1 Ventura came about as a logical extension of Lockheed's successful Model 14 airliner which, through modifications, became the RAF's Hudson bomber. Although a bit obsolete by European conflict standards, the Hudson was a tough bird and better and more advanced than many British designs fulfilling the same mission. On 23 June 1938, the British Purchasing Comission issued an order for 200 Hudsons, thus providing the RAF with a much needed combat aircraft, and Lockheed with vital orders that would allow for expansion.

Due to the less than enthusiastic acceptance of the Lockheed Model 14 airliner by American operators, the company decided to stop production of the aircraft and concentrate on the Model 18 which, although looking a great deal like the Model 14, featured numerous improvements and was given the name Lodestar. Carrying either 15 or 18 passengers depending on airline preference, the type was created with more enthusiasm but could not break the hold that the Douglas DC-3 had gained. In order to explore all possible avenues, Lockheed presented a militarized, on paper, variant of the Model 18 to the British. The new aircraft could use its standard powerplants or could be equipped with other units, depending on preference. The RAF liked the idea of an aircraft equipped with the Pratt & Whitney R-2800 of 1850 hp (the engine would dramatically 'grow' in power output as it was developed) and in May 1940 a contract was initiated for the delivery of Ventura bombers. Production would be handled by Lockheed's Vega Airplane Company subsidiary, which was also at Burbank

Having learned from the Hudson, Lockheed and the RAF improved the Ventura's armour, systems and armament. The aircraft still retained the hideous Boulton-Paul turret which brought a new meaning to the term 'drag', but the unit was moved further forward to give an increased field of fire for the puny twin .303 in machne guns on the initial aircraft (increased to four on later production machines). Two further guns were mounted on a swivel mount in the nose while two more effective .50 calibre Brownings were fixed in the upper nose decking. A bomb load of 2500 lb could be carried and even though the aircraft had a heavier weight than the Model 18, good short field performance was still available courtesy of all that extra horsepower, and from the efficiency of the Fowler flaps.

As RAF camouflaged machines rolled down the production line, both the Army and Navy ordered similar aircraft, while the RAF increased their order under the new Lend-Lease agreement and Lockheed Vega would go on to build 3028 aircraft in the Ventura/B-34/PV-1 production run.

The RAF was pleased with the Ventura, even though nine of the aircraft were destroyed and a further 37 damaged out of 47 taking part in a low-level daylight attack against a factory in The Netherlands on 6 December

...for PROTECTION today and PROGRESS tomorrow

LOOK TO Lockheed FOR LEADERSHIP in both!

Above The PV-1/PV-2 series of patrol bombers worked long and hard for the US Navy, and when aircraft were surplused from NAS Litchfield Park, Arizona, the weary twin-engined warriors were snapped up by civilian buyers who wanted to keep them working. While many airframes went to rebuilders who converted the Lockheeds to sleek executive transports, the majority went to operators who used the craft as fire bombers, bug sprayers or cargo haulers. Photographed from under the nose of a weary B-17 fire bomber in October 1985, this line-up of PV-2 Harpoon sprayers waits to go under the auction hammer at the Globe Air facility at Falcon Field in Mesa, Arizona. This event was probably the last true warbird auction where airframes were available at somewhat reasonable prices. The Harpoons went from $7500 to $20,000 depending on airframe, engine time, etc

Left After purchase at the Globe Air auction, PV-2 N7483C's R-2800s receive attention prior to a ferry flight. This aircraft is equipped with underwing spray bars as well as wing tip dispensers for fire ant poison. The fire ant plagues the south and southwest and PV-2s helped alleviate the pesky creatures during the 1960s and 1970s, before environmental considerations eliminated the majority of poisons being utilized

1942. The Ventura, in a number of variants, would operate with the RAF and other Commonwealth air forces throughout the war.

During the first months of 1942, the Navy got the Army to transfer complete responsibility for anti-submarine warfare to the Navy, but the service was short on aircraft. Up until this point, the Navy had placed great reliance on flying boats, but land-based patrol bombers were rapidly gaining favour, so the Navy got the Army to relinquish production on their B-34s and transfer the line to the Navy as the PV-1. In order to accommodate the patrol mission, the PV-1s had internal fuel supply increased and provisions added for underwing fuel tanks. Power came from dependable P&W R-2800-31s capable of 2000 hp each. Armament comprised two fixed .50 calibres in the nose upper decking, with two similar units in a dorsal turret and two .30 calibre Brownings on a swivel mount in the belly. The bomb bay was increased to hold 3000 lbs of bombs or one torpedo. Later production PV-1s were fitted with a nose pack carrying a further three .50 calibre weapons and underwing hardpoints for eight high velocity aerial rockets.

The PV-1 made its maiden flight on 3 November 1942 and Lockheed Vega went on to deliver 1600 machines to the Navy, with production ending in May 1944. With its long range, good weapons load and rugged dependability, the PV-1 went on to see a great deal of action with the Navy and Marines (modified PV-1s equipped the USMC's first night fighter squadron, VMF(N)-531) and saw far-ranging action from the Atlantic to Alaska to the Pacific. Even though the PV-1 faced enemy action on a daily

Below Ground crew attach the slurry hose to the belly tank of Harpoon N6651D Tanker 40, BuNo 151503, at Omak, Washington, during August 1973. The Harpoon made an efficient aerial tanker, its R-2800s providing the pilot with plenty of power, which is always useful when operating in the hazardous environment of fire bombing

basis, the type received little press, even though the battles it waged were every bit as deadly as its more famous counterparts.

After the Navy had taken over the PV-1 production line for patrol bomber duties, the service began discussions with Lockheed to create an improved variant that would be completely optimized for the patrol mission. The resulting aircraft was Vega Model 15, which had an increased wing span, much larger vertical tails, increased fuel capacity, increased bomb load and defensive armament. The bomber retained the same R-2800s, even though the weight had gone up, but the reduced overall speed was, the Navy felt, compensated by longer range, more punch and better handling qualities. Designated PV-2 and named Harpoon, the first example flew from Burbank on 3 December 1943.

Testing of the PV-2 soon revealed a major problem – the wing began to distort and buckle. The most immediate solution was to decrease the span by six feet, but this did not correct the problem and a complete new wing design had to be created, thus greatly delaying production schedules. By the end of 1944, the Navy had accepted only 69 PV-2s, but once the problems were corrected, the Harpoon became a very efficient combat

Left Certainly the 'meanest' looking of all executive Ventura/Harpoon conversions is the mighty Howard 500. So much rework went into the design that it was certificated as a 'new' aircraft, but the machine's ancestry is obvious. Dee Howard of San Antonio, Texas, pretty well did away with the aircraft's fuselage and installed a custom-built pressurized unit instead, while two CB variants of the R-2800 provided 2500 hp each and had modified cowlings and four blade props. Definitely the Learjet of its day, the Howard 500 was a limited production aircraft and, because of its speed and range, became very popular with drug runners during the 1970s, and many examples were lost pursuing this lucrative activity. Howard 500 N130P is seen at Chandler Memorial Airport, Arizona, on 26 October 1990

machine. Lockheed Vega would go on to build 500 PV-2s. VPB-139 took the Harpoon into combat for the first time during March 1945 when they went to work in the very hostile Aleutians. The PV-2, once the problems had been rectified, was an excellent aircraft and greatly appreciated by its crews. In fact, both PV-1s and PV-2s often took on Japanese Zeros and defeated the enemy in a telling manner. The Japanese learned that the twin-engined Lockheeds were not to be treated with distain.

Venturas and Harpoons were also supplied to America's allies during and after the war, the PV-2 continuing to serve well into the 1950s. After frontline service, many PV-2s were supplied to Reserve units and at one time equipped 11 squadrons. The Korean War saw PV-2s brought out of storage at Litchfield Park and put into airworthy status to bolster America's aerial armada, even though the type was not used in the bloody conflict.

By the late 1950s, many PV-1s and PV-2s were put up for sale on the civilian market and the aircraft found ready buyers. Some machines were smuggled to Africa and South America, where they were used in mercenary operations, while it is rumoured that the Central Intelligence Agency also utilized the Harpoon to good effect in some of the more remote trouble spots of the early 1960s. A great deal of success had been enjoyed by Dee Howard and Bill Lear in converting Model 18s into high-speed executive transports, and thought was given to doing the same thing to Venturas and Harpoons now available for civil use.

Quite a few of the twins were sold as surplus, and at least 140 Harpoons alone got onto the civil register, even though many were never actually

Right With the big R-2800s humming along, highly-modified Howard PV-2 N7428C is seen cruising near Titusville, Florida, during March 1986, with the Space Shuttle assembly building prominent in the background. The PV-2 was taken to Howard by its owners for conversion to a freighter to haul rare plants to the States from Latin America. In 1965, Howard started work on the airframe, gutting the interior, installing a right side fuselage cargo door and extending the fuselage by four feet. The aircraft's new mission did not last long as the owners went bankrupt, and the twin wound up being used as a drug runner, before being impounded and eventually purchased by Richard Mitchell of New Iberia, Louisiana

converted. The myriad modifications involved would fill this volume as almost each executive aircraft was custom-built to the buyer's specialized requirements. Bill Lear used aerodynamic improvements to the Lodestar to create the Learstar which, while using the same Model 18 powerplants, was able to achieve a top speed of 321 mph with 12 passengers seated in comfort. Dee Howard had more modifications and the Howard 250 retained the Model 18's standard Wright R-1820-56s of 1350 hp each giving a top speed of 310 mph, while carrying 10 to 12 passengers. The Model 350 utilized the PV-1 as the basis of its airframe, and the first production 350 flew on 1 April 1962. Powered by P&W R-2800 CB-17s of 2500 hp, the aircraft could seat 10 to 14 passengers and cruise at 315 mph. The Howard Model 500, while clearly based on the PV-1/PV-2, was certificated by the FAA as a new aircraft on 20 February 1963, and the twin featured a fail-safe pressurized fuselage with the same passenger capability as the 350. The engines were P&W R-2800 CB-17s fitted with four-bladed propellers, and the aircraft had a maximum cruise speed of 389 mph. The prototype Howard 500 first flew during September 1959, followed by the first production model on 15 March 1960.

The Howards proved to be the 'Learjets' of their day, offering fast and relatively comfortable transportation for the businessman that did not want to depend on airline schedules. Their moment of fame proved to be rather fleeting since the new business jets, led by the Lear, were beginning to appear on the market, and the Howards, along with PV-1/PV-2 conversions offered by several other companies, began to fade into second

Above The finest Harpoon rebuild, and one of the finest of all warbird restorations, was PV-2D N7250C belonging to Doug Lacey. BuNo 84061 had been a fire ant bomber before being purchased by Lacey, who went through the entire airframe, rebuilding and adding authentic equipment including a Martin upper turret, rockets, working bomb bay with 500 lb bombs, original radios, radar, etc. Lacey had finished the aircraft in postwar US Naval Reserve markings and the bomber is seen over Lake Tahoe in June 1990. On 29 September 1990, while making a series of passes and steep pull-ups over a seaplane fly-in at Clearlake, California, the Harpoon entered a high speed stall and plunged into the lake, killing Lacey and his seven passengers instantly

and third line operations. The aircraft, with their high speed, good load carrying ability and long range, often became drug runners and the majority of the production run was expended in this manner. Today, a flying Howard in good condition is a rarity.

The majority of the civil Harpoons were not converted into 'board room bombers', but a couple of conversions did take place including the rather

Right doors opening, PV-2 N7265C, BuNo 37396, turns into a left bank, illustrating details such as the oil cooler intakes, nose gun pack for three .50 calibre Brownings and ventral gun position. This aircraft has been restored back to military condition by the American Military Heritage Foundation in Indianapolis, Indiana, from its former sprayer configuration, and is seen over Geneseo on 16 August 1991. The larger vertical tails on the PV-2 Harpoon helped increase directional stability over the earlier Ventura. Only 500 Harpoons were built by Vega, but the type went on to have a long postwar career with the Naval Air Reserve and, later, civilian operators

elegant Oakland Airmotive Centaurus, which met the light of day during 1958. Modified to carry between eight and 14 passengers, the fuselage had been heavily modified to accept pressurization, while the entire airframe received aerodynamic improvements including new cowls. The Centaurus had a maximum speed of 328 mph, but met with little to no interest and, apparently, only two were sold.

Most civil PV-2s were simply and quickly modified into workhorses by the addition of bomb bay borate tanks and spray gear that could be used for agricultural work or for insect eradication. Once again, the Harpoon provided years of essential but little-known work. By the mid-1980s, these aircraft were becoming available on the warbird market, and many were snapped up by eager collectors since the prices were refreshingly low and the parts supply high. Since then, several aircraft have been returned to their original military configuration and are very popular on the airshow circuit. As of July 1993, Hirth Air Tankers in Buffalo, Wyoming, was still operating seven Harpoons – two as tankers and the rest as sprayers – so this Lockheed classic still has lots of life left in it.

Hot Stuff – the attractive nose art on Harpoon N7265C. Although the PV-1/PV-2 series saw heavy combat during World War 2, the type is not well represented on the warbird circuit, but fortunately restorations like this one are helping to correct the balance and illustrate the importance of patrol aviation during the war

Lockheed PV, B-34 and Ventura/Harpoon

Origin: Vega Aircraft Corporation, Burbank, California
Type: Bomber and reconnaissance aircraft
Engines: Two 2000 hp Pratt & Whitney R-2800-31 Double Wasp 18-cylinder radial
Dimensions: Span (V) 65 ft 6 in (19.96 m); (H) 75 ft (22.86 m); length 51 ft 5 in to 51 ft 9 in (15.77 m); height 13 ft 2 in (3.9 m) to 14 ft 1 in (4.29 m); wing area (V) 551 sq ft (51.19 m²), (H) 686 sq ft (63.73 m²).
Weights: Empty (V) 19,373 lbs (8788 kg), (H) about 24,000 lbs (10,886 kg); maximum (V) 31,077 lbs (14,097 kg), (H) 40,000 (18,144 kg)
Performance: Maximum speed (V) 300 mph (483 km/h), (H) 282 mph (454 km/h); maximum range with max bombload (all) about 900 miles (1448 km)
Armament: See text.
History: First fight (RAF) 31 July 1941; service delivery (RAF) June 1942, (Navy) December 1942; final delivery (H) 1945